Anonymous

Republican Superstitions as Illustrated in the Political History of America

Anonymous

Republican Superstitions as Illustrated in the Political History of America

ISBN/EAN: 9783337202514

Printed in Europe, USA, Canada, Australia, Japan

Cover: Foto ©ninafisch / pixelio.de

More available books at **www.hansebooks.com**

REPUBLICAN SUPERSTITIONS

AS ILLUSTRATED IN THE POLITICAL

HISTORY OF AMERICA

BY

MONCURE D. CONWAY, M.A.

AUTHOR OF 'TESTIMONIES CONCERNING SLAVERY'
AND
'THE EARTHWARD PILGRIMAGE'

LONDON
HENRY S. KING & CO., 65 CORNHILL
1872

CONTENTS.

	PAGE
LETTER TO M. LOUIS BLANC	v
LETTER FROM M. LOUIS BLANC	xi
THE STATE SUPERSTITION	1
THE TWO CHAMBERS	18
THE PRESIDENT	79
DELUSIVE DIPLOMACY	119
CONCLUSION	129

To M. Louis Blanc, Deputy for Paris.

My dear M. Louis Blanc,

Permit me, in admiration of your genius and courage, and of the devotion of these unwaveringly through all the vicissitudes of your country to the principles of justice and liberty, to inscribe your name on the first page of this little work.

In doing so I add a brief explanation of the motives which have led me to prepare and to publish it.

Some time ago, when a vigorous arraignment of the English Monarchy by a Baronet and Member of Parliament had given fresh impulse to the Republican agitation in this country, I was conscious, as an American, of profound misgivings concerning certain features of the discussion which occurred. It was not that the Republican principles which ten years ago I brought with me from my native country had become in any degree weakened; on the contrary, every year passed in nearer observation of European systems has served to confirm them. My misgivings arose at the almost unquestioning uniformity with which the organic forms of the American Republic were accepted as representing the model of self-governing society. To substitute a Senate for the House of Lords and a President for the Queen appeared to be the fixed aim of the great majority of those who avowed Republican principles. Having been these many years convinced that the Senate and the Presidency are serious anomalies in the American Republic, and that the healthy progress of that country has been impeded by them, I availed myself of an invitation to deliver an address before the London Dialectical Society to briefly indicate my views in this regard. In that address I spoke of the normal belief that popular government naturally organised itself into two branches of Legislature and a President as a 'Republican

Superstition,' and though the phrase was sharply criticised, it still seems to me a true one.

France has advanced to the momentous and critical phase which is now absorbing the attention and exciting the sympathy of the most earnest and thoughtful friends of human liberty throughout the world. Republicanism in some form has become the necessity of France. That the lifelong Monarchist who now presides over that nation should be showing a determination to build up the Republic is a sufficient indication that the forces acting in that direction are irresistible. The great problem has become now the form in which the Republic shall be organised. And knowing that the law of mechanics that a machine is no stronger than its weakest part, is equally true of political constitutions, it can only be with anxiety that an American can hear the many rumours that the President of the French Republic is aiming, not only to preserve the Presidential office, but also to secure the addition of a second legislative Chamber to the Government over whose organisation he has such controlling power. It is these rumours which give an ominous sound to the address of the President of the Council-General of Avignon in September last, wherein, speaking as the organ of M. Thiers, he said : 'The President trusts that the French Republic will one day become a worthy sister of the Republic of the United States.' There are incidents in the early relations between France and America of which the citizens of both countries have every reason to be proud, which have long invested the governmental forms of the United States with a charm for French statesmen and a prestige for the French people. The critical admiration of De Tocqueville, and the less discriminating eulogium of M. Laboulaye, have contributed to that general satisfaction with which the holding up of the Transatlantic Republic as a model by the President's representative at Avignon has been received by the Republicans of France. It may seem unpatriotic for an American to deprecate any such fate for France as that which M. Thiers promises; but I believe that the love of one's country which seeks to correct its faults, and to prevent those faults from misleading other nations, is truer than that whose motto is ' Our country, right or wrong.' A patriot cannot serve his country better than to do his best to purge it of error, and to make its influence an unmixed benefit to mankind.

I may be asked why it is that, if the evils to which I call attention in these pages really exist, they have not already been subjects for denunciation and discussion among the distinguished statesmen and political thinkers of the United States. Why should it be left to an unofficial and obscure American in London to discover them ? I answer, I have not discovered them. I have often heard similar expressions and criticisms fall from the lips of Americans at whose feet I have rejoiced to sit. But it is true that I find myself unable to fortify my positions by printed essays, or by Congressional debates. The reason why I cannot bring authorities is, so far as the statesmen and politicians of the United States are concerned, somewhat humiliating, and so obvious, that I am almost tempted to pass them by. The American politician does not criticise the Senatorial or Presidential office, because he hopes to fill both. That the great reformers who have signalised their devotion to a noble cause by refusing all official connection with the Government, so long as its flag protected slavery, may be explained by the consideration that they have had to pass their lives in the thick of battle, and could hardly spare attention to enquiries which, apparently, were not urged upon them by the matter in hand. I say *apparently*, for I shall show in the following pages that the struggle in which they fought so bravely was not only prolonged, but finally transferred, from the arena of debate to that of war by the constitutional defects which I have felt impelled to press upon the attention of European Republicans.

I am, my dear M. Blanc,
&c. &c.
M. D. CONWAY.

PARIS: October 7, 1872.

MY DEAR MR. CONWAY,

As early as 1846 I published a paper in which I endeavoured to show that the establishment of a second Chamber was fraught with unmitigated evils, and afforded but a sham remedy for the political dangers it was intended to ward off.

By the end of 1848, just at the time when Louis Napoleon Bonaparte was coming forward as a candidate for the Presidential office, I thought it my duty to point out the direful consequences likely to flow from the election of a President. The solemn warning I then gave to my countrymen was expressed as follows :—' Whenever a man and an Assembly stand face to face, that Assembly brings with it a 10 Août, and that man has behind him an 18 Brumaire.'

But, as you have rightly observed, there are political as well as religious superstitions, nor are the former more easily uprooted than the latter. At the time alluded to it seemed next to impossible that there should be a Republic without a

President. A strange aberration this—more especially on the part of the French, as they had been taught by experience how readily a President or Consul is turned into an Emperor.

However, the warning was disregarded, and on the 2nd of December, 1851, we had to undergo the unspeakable humiliation of another 18 Brumaire. My prediction was thus fulfilled, even sooner than I expected.

Whether we shall know how to turn to account the lesson we have repeatedly received, remains to be seen. I hope it will be so. Certain it is that now-a-days many are they in the Republican party who consider the Presidential office as a mere stepping-stone to ascend the throne. If others have some doubt left as to the necessity, both of a President and a second Chamber, it is because they are under the impression that that system works well in the United States. To correct such an error is to do good service to the cause of Republican institutions.

Faithfully yours,

LOUIS BLANC.

REPUBLICAN SUPERSTITIONS.

THE STATE SUPERSTITION.

I.

A SUPERSTITION is any belief not based upon evidence.

The term is indeed ordinarily associated with unfounded religious beliefs or legends, because religion is a region from which reason has so long been barred—whilst admitted in all other departments of inquiry—that the preponderant number of superstitions are found in that direction. Nevertheless, in the proportionate degree in which human concerns approximate religion in importance, superstitions adhere to them. In medicine, where physical life and death are concerned, it may be tracked from the prescription of the rustic herbalist to the practice of professional men. And in social and political affairs, where home, property, and person are involved, the reformer has to encounter at every step institutions which seem inexpugnable simply because they are based upon conventional prejudice or sentiment, and are therefore not subject to the tests of reason with which they have no ground in common.

And this is one thing which all superstitions, whether political or religious, have in common: they rest upon mere authority. This authority, whether it have visible representative or be the more powerful sanction of immemorial custom, reflects simply the degree of timidity, ignorance, or mental indolence, existing in those who submit to it.

Superstitions agree also in this—they subsist only under the condition that the age or the individual holding them shall be quite unconscious of them. A superstition is no sooner recognised as such than it is either rejected or becomes an hypocrisy. The freest mind, therefore, cannot be sure that no superstition survives in it. Lord Bacon can see the idols of many caves; but his inductive philosophy reveals no absurdity in his recommendation of 'whelps or young healthy boys applied to the stomach,' as an astringent. Lord Herbert of Cherbury is quite unaware of the smile he is preparing for posterity by praying for —and, as he believes, receiving—a revelation from heaven authorising the publication of his work demonstrating the impossibility of a revelation from heaven.

Fortunately, however, we do not all hold the same superstitions. We can each detect the other's delusion, and can bravely unmask every idol but our own. This is the security that each point in the fabric of superstition will in turn feel the fatal touch of scientific thought, and crumble away.

II.

The men who framed the Constitution of the United States were, perhaps, above all their contemporaries in the world, free from both religious and political superstitions. The country planted in the principle of a Church without a Bishop and a State without a King, had finally produced a generation of leaders determined to have a State without a Church—nay, without even the faintest recognition of the Deity or of Christianity. Free-thinkers in such matters, they were also relieved to a remarkable degree from prejudices in favour of the political institutions amid which they had been trained. In the first glow of revolutionary enthusiasm the traditional institutions of England had been quietly ignored, and in forming their first Confederation the original thirteen States almost without argument constituted a single House of Congress, and, quite ignoring monarchical associations, appointed an Executive Committee to carry on the government at such times as the Congress was not in Session.

Nevertheless, the past was not to be amputated in this summary way. The tradition that property, land, and rank, were to be weighed against man in representation, which had given to England its House of Lords and its representative knights of shires in the House of Commons, had survived in the first union formed by the Puritans of New England. There we find the government consisting of delegates from congregations of pilgrims settled in different centres, each of these congregations having an equal number of votes, whatever their relative size. And when in place of these congregations there stood thirteen States, several of them hardly larger than some counties in the others, they based their Confederation on the assumed sanctity of the state survey-lines. Rhode Island must cast the same number of votes in congress as New York!

How were these States formed? Why was New York large and Rhode Island small? Why should not the American people have partitioned out their territory into a convenient number of districts? The States had been developed from various historic centres, and although their interests were, certainly at that time, identical, and their boundaries scarcely defined, the local sentiment was as yet quite too strong for the formation of a large and earnest nationality. The union they did frame was not one of sympathy, but one formed under the sense of separate weakness in presence of a foreign enemy. Its brief duration showed that the State was everything, the solidarity of the people nothing; and after a life enfeebled by inter-state jealousies, its inharmonious existence terminated.

This feeling of the sanctity of state-lines was itself strangely tinged with superstition; at least, it seems to have been originally due more to hereditary notions than to any positive differences of interest. While it gave each State one vote in the Congress, the republican principle had to be satisfied with the right of States to send a larger or less number of delegates in proportion to their population, this variation of power being strictly limited to talking.

The emphasis given to geographical and local patriotism was gradually productive of separate interests. And when these began to bear heavily upon the bond which united the first Confederation—a bond already weakened as the apprehensions of foreign invasion which had formed it began to vanish—it broke asunder. The weakness that proved fatal was the absence of any sufficient central authority, which was but the counterpart of the preponderant provincial pride and local selfishness euphemistically called state sovereignty or state-independence.

III.

It was under these circumstances that the ablest men in America were appointed by the several States to meet together and devise some means of so amending the articles of the Confederation as to form a national union.

From the first it was evident that the one great problem they had to solve was how to harmonise the feeling of state-independence with the purposes of a general government sufficiently strong to make a real nation. Some of the truest and wisest statesmen saw and declared that the only means of securing a real union was to abolish the States, and partition the territory into districts based on population, and changeable with its subsequent growth or variation. They proposed that these districts should have their local assemblies to deal with clearly defined classes of local interests, and that they should be represented in one national legislative Chamber. Had their insight guided the majority of the Convention, it is needless to say that it would have saved the United States from the long and shameful reign of slavery, and from the fearful civil war in which that reign reached its climax and its end.

But those who held these views were very few, and they only suggested their views with bated breath ; for it was plain that the States were jealous of their so-called sovereignty, though it is certain that they never really had any separate sovereignty, having previously been dependencies of Great Britain and having achieved a common independence as united colonies.

The struggle in the Constitutional Convention turned practically upon no such radical project as the extinction or modification of the existing States, but upon their relative power in the new Government. The strength of State jealousy was naturally strongest in the smallest ones, and a representative of the most insignificant of these declared in the Convention, that his State would offer its hand to a foreign power, if it were sought to bind its will by the controlling power of the larger States.

The result was a compromise. It was finally agreed that in the new union there should be, as it were, a double set of States. The old historical colonies should remain to continue their idea that the soil within their survey-lines was more sacred than any outside of them, and that a system of governors, legislatures, and courts should be built up upon these; also that they should own a special branch of Congress, the Senate, in which each State should have an equal number of delegates, and an equal vote, whatever might be the differences in their size or population. By the side of this system it was agreed that there should be a national Republican Government, whose States should be equal districts apportioned throughout the country on the basis of population; and that these should have a central branch of their own. It was only to a national Government so constituted that the States were willing to surrender their sovereignty, which each had claimed after the attainment of their independence of Great Britain, by united effort.

But just so soon as some of the States found, in process of time, that some of their separate interests were not adopted as the chief objects of the National Government, the surrendered State-sovereignty was theoretically resuscitated under the name of 'State-rights,' and they claimed a sufficient supremacy over the union to destroy it.

Under the union thus constituted there had been gradually formed a sufficient consolidation of commercial and other interests, to render a threat of withdrawal from it on the part of any State or States, the most formidable that could be made; and, although the secession clearly did not exist within the provisions of the national compact, the disasters which it was foreseen must attend such an effort, led to the complete and cowardly surrender of the United States Government, for more than a generation, to the tyranny of the slaveholding interest.

In these days when the almost superstitious horror of what is vaguely termed Centralisation has to a large extent blinded public men to the fact that the good or the evil of it chiefly depends upon the kind of centre in which power is organised, it seems to me sufficient attention has not been given to the illustration of the dangers of extreme decentralisation, in a Republic, furnished by the history of the United States.

Through the degree of power left by the framers of the Constitution to the several States, each of these was made into a centre of political intrigue and ambition, and was encouraged to rivalry of, and finally to encroachment upon the powers of the general Government. They held in the Senate a power to negative the will of the whole people, as expressed through their representatives in the popular branch of the Legislature; and however the millions of the United States might vote, they could only bring to bear at the final decision on any measure the same amount of legislative power as small communities ruled by local interests. The entire power in the Slave States resided in a slaveholding aristocracy of three hundred thousand; but these spread out through fifteen States were able—their votes being reinforced by the threats of disunion which secured the alliance of senators from contiguous States—to control the entire Union. They were able to plunge the country into what was called the Mexican War, but which really was a raid to rob a neighbouring country of certain territory desired for the purpose of extending slavery and giving it more votes in the Senate; they were able to devote the national forces to the work of crushing the extension of free labour into north-western territories; they made the free States a hunting-ground on which the officers of the United States were compelled to hunt down and capture negroes seeking their liberty; they were able to corrupt by threats and bribes the pulpit and the press of the entire nation, and to render it a danger for any man to defend the commonest principles of justice or humanity.

Out of this abyss into which the system

founded on colonies had thrown the country, the United States was enabled to emerge only at the cost of the best blood in the nation. The free cities of Germany and Italy lost their liberties by the multiplication of principalities: the free people of America were only saved from a similar fate by the fact that, after all, the monarchical features which their Constitution had retained proved to be of but transient strength, compared with the elements which were purely Republican.

During the late civil war in America, we heard many prophets anticipating the event, and already eagerly pointing to the downfall of the Union as the natural result of Republicanism. But at no time since its foundation was the Republic ever threatened by anything but the lingering elements of Monarchy which it had unhappily retained.

The party which carried this State system to an extreme—and by which the nation was ruled until plunged by it into civil war—was called by a singular misnomer, Democratic. Their democracy consisted in insisting on the equality of notoriously unequal surveyed lands, to the sacrifice of all real and human equality.

Unquestionably there is need that real local

interests shall be carefully attended to, and it is necessary that between the nation and the town, or even the family, there shall be a fine gradation of self-government, so far as such interests are concerned. The planet may have freedom of revolution on its own axis as well as its relationship to the solar system. Such municipal or local self-government is only endangered, however, when it is empowered to deal with affairs which belong to the general welfare. Its own ultimate security depends on its limitation, and on its submission to the larger need of the nation.

It is, above all, necessary for the solidarity of a Republic that in the adjustment of legislative districts their boundaries should not be coincident with any antiquarian or historical lines which would foster clannish pride or recollections. It seems, for example, an object of legitimate reform that the English Parliament should distribute some of its work among local legislatures; but to resuscitate for this the ancient kingdoms of Scotland, Ireland, and Wales would be simple suicide.

Could there be a more cruel concession made by England to Ireland than that very Home Rule for which so earnest a demand is now made? Whether England should concede complete independence to Ireland may be a question; but to raise up in Ireland ambitions that at some point must be checked, to give embodiment to aspirations and interests which can no sooner reach their development than they will be certainly crushed, were the gift of weak indulgence, and by no means that of true generosity. For every concession the Northern people made to 'State-sovereignty' in the South several thousand Southerners had to be slain in the end.

It may be asked, What shall be the rule of adjustment between local interests and national interests? Who shall decide whether a particular tax is one that should be justly controlled by a national Legislature or by a distinct assembly? To this I reply that the only security against any encroachment of the whole on the parts, or of the parts on the whole, must rest, as it seems to me, upon the three fundamental principles which the constitutional fathers of the United States laid as corner-stones of Republican Government.

1. That local self-government shall be organised in such a way as that no district shall have any artificial superiority over another; and that such

district governments shall be made sufficiently flexible to undergo such modifications as growth or other changes in a community may render desirable.

2. These districts to be represented in a national Congress, which should be chosen by the entire people, pledged to hold merely local interests subordinate to the welfare of the whole nation.

3. There should be a written Constitution, clearly defining the powers both of the district and of the national legislatures. This Constitution should have a Supreme Court for its final interpretation, and an Executive Committee for its enforcement.

Having devised this simple Republican system, the founders of the American Constitution were compelled to compromise it, and, in order to establish the Union at all, to submit that it should be overlaid by the antiquated and fictitious State system. Not only did they recognise the old and accidental boundaries of colonies as representing States, but they gave to these communities complete control of one equal branch of the National Legislature; and allotted them also a power over the election of the Executive, which virtually deprived the people of the right to elect that officer. The representative districts do indeed vote for the President, but not directly; they vote for a list of State electors, and those named on the chosen list repair to Washington, and record their vote for the candidate they were elected to support. It follows, however, from this thrusting of the so-called State between the people and the presidential election, that the Executive may be chosen by a minority of the nation. For one State may have had its list of electors chosen by a bare majority of its citizens, while another may have elected its list almost unanimously. All the votes of the minority, however large, are thrown away simply because they could not elect their list of electors; on the other hand, all the surplus votes in a State above a bare majority are equally thrown away. Thus, suppose Ohio, Virginia, and Maryland have between them to elect A or B to be President, and cast votes as follows:—

	A	B
Ohio.	250,001	250,000
Virginia.	240,000	230,000
Maryland.	220,000	250,000

B has a majority of 19,999, and is—defeated. Ohio and Virginia have returned A's electors. As a matter of fact there have been several minority Presidents in the history of the United States.

It was, indeed, as will be shown further on, a grievous error that the election of the Executive should have been remitted to the people at all; but the evils consequent upon that error are only intensified where the choice may perhaps not even represent the genuine voice of the people.

—Such then, in part, has been the story of the State-superstition in America. But only in part; for the degree to which the growth of a high public feeling, a large national soul, has been impeded, cannot be estimated. For the first hundred years of American independence, we have heard men proudly calling themselves Virginians and Carolinians, and even Bostonians, but it is a recent experience to hear it said in the same tone, 'I am an American.'

THE TWO CHAMBERS.

I.

It was not at all necessary, when it was determined that the States should have a distinct representation in the Congress, that they should also have a separate House. The State deputies might have sat in the same Chamber with the representatives of the people just as the knights of shires do with other members in the House of Commons. The separation of them into two Houses was accepted upon the precedent of the British Parliament, and on no real grounds whatever. Of the original States, at the time of the adoption of the Constitution, two had but one legislative Chamber each, and the Confederation had no more. When the proposition was made to divide the Congress into two branches, three States, the great State of New York among them, recorded their votes against it, and the delegation of another, Maryland, was equally divided on the subject. There seems, however, to have been very little discussion of the matter, which was quite overshadowed by the incomparable urgency of the only question—the relative power of the States and the general Government—which really was discussed in the Convention. The debates were in secret, and we have but brief notes of them; but a passage in the minutes jotted down by one of the members, Chief Justice Yates, of New York, no doubt tells the whole story :—'May 31, 1787. The 3rd resolve to wit, "That the National Legislature ought to consist of two branches," was taken into consideration, and without any debate, agreed to.' To this Judge Yates adds, in brackets: 'N.B. As a previous resolution had already been agreed to, to have a supreme Legislature, I could not see any objection to its being in two branches.' So lightly was a step taken which has proved to be of momentous consequence to America!

Curtis, the generally accepted historian of the American Constitution, has a passage on this subject which no doubt accurately represents the average ignorance and traditional sentiment which prevailed to establish the two Houses in America. He says: 'The needful harmony and completeness of the scheme, according to the genius of the

Anglo-American liberty, required the division of the Legislature. Doubtless a single Council or Chamber can promulgate decrees and enact laws; but it had never been the habit of the people of America, as it never had been the habit of their ancestors for at least a period of more than five centuries, to regard a single Chamber as favourable to liberty or to wise legislation. The separation into two Chambers of the Lords Spiritual and Temporal and the Commons, in the English Constitution, does not seem to have originated in a difference of personal rank so much as in their position as separate estates of the realm. All the orders might have been voted promiscuously in one House, and just as effectually signified the assent or dissent of Parliament to any measure proposed; but the practice of making the assent of Parliament to consist in the concurrent and separate action of the two estates, though difficult to be traced to its origin in any distinct purpose or cause, became confirmed by the growing importance of the Commons, by their jealousy and vigilance, and by the controlling position which they finally assumed. As Parliament gradually proceeded to its present constitution, and the separate rights and privileges of the two Houses became established, it was found that the practice of discussing a measure in two assemblies, composed of different persons, holding their seats by a different tenure, and representing different orders of the State, was in the highest degree conducive to the security of the subject and to sound legislation.'

So far as any clear impression arises from the hazy annals of the earliest parliamentary government in England, it is that the king called upon the leading noblemen of the realm to become his guests for a time for purposes of consultation, feasting them meanwhile in grand style. This was the only Parliament. To this assembly come groups of petitioners, deputations from the people; and these, in order that their requests may be presented with some kind of regularity, must needs organise their assemblies, and appoint some mouth-piece or Speaker, now represented by the most silent official bearing that name. For it is in this group of deputations that we must recognise the future Commons' House, which for a time sat in the presence of the Parliament of Peers, until the latter thought it beneath their dignity to sit beside those of lower rank. The separation probably occurred at the time when the Commoners ceased to be a mere crowd of petitioners to their lordships, and showed signs of becoming a normal element in the government. The House of Peers represented the supremacy of the aristocratic and clerical classes, of which the Crown was the head; the Commons represented the degree to which the people had managed to extort the first point, recognition of their existence, and of the simplest rights implied in that existence.

It is a notable fact that, while the founders of the American Constitution were taking up this relic of feudalism and clothing it with formidable power, the English nation was already preparing the forces which were to reduce the House of Lords to the secondary position it now occupies.

II.

After reading the statement of the American historian, it may assist us to ponder the following from one of the ablest of recent writers on the English Constitution, Mr. Bagehot :—' The evil of two co-equal Houses of distinct natures is obvious. Each

House can stop all legislation, and yet some legislation may be necessary. At this moment we have the best instance of this which could be conceived. The Upper House of our Victorian Constitution, representing the rich wool-growers, has disagreed with the Lower Assembly, and most business is suspended. But for a most curious stratagem the machine of government would stand still. Most Constitutions have committed this blunder. The two most remarkable Republican institutions in the world commit it. In both the American and the Swiss Constitutions the Upper House has as much authority as the second; it could produce the maximum of impediment, the dead-lock, if it liked. If it does not do so, it is owing, not to the goodness of the legal constitution, but to the discreetness of the members of the Chamber. In both these Constitutions this dangerous provision is defended by a peculiar doctrine with which I have nothing to do now. It is said there must be in a Federal Government some institution, some authority, somebody possessing a veto, in which the separate States composing the Confederation are all equal. I confess this doctrine has to me no self-evidence, and it is assumed, but not proved. The

State of Delaware is *not* equal in power or influence to the State of New York, and you cannot make it so by giving it an equal veto in an Upper Chamber. The history of such an institution is most natural. A little State will like, and must like, to see some memorial mark of its old independence preserved in the Constitution by which that independence is extinguished. But it is one thing for an institution to be natural, another for it to be expedient. If indeed it be that a Federal Government compels the erection of an Upper Chamber of conclusive and co-ordinate authority, it is one more in addition to the many other inherent defects of that kind of government. It may be necessary to have the blemish, but it is a blemish just as much.'

Mr. Bagehot then shows that since the Reform Act of 1832, when the House of Lords for the last time really tried conclusions with the House of Commons and was compelled to yield, it has not even had a pretension to being an equal branch of the government. 'The House of Lords has become a revising and suspending House. It can alter Bills; it can reject Bills on which the House of Commons is not yet thoroughly in earnest, upon which the nation is not yet determined. Their veto is a sort of hypothetical veto. They say, We reject your bill for this once, or these twice, or these thrice; but if you keep on sending it up, at last we won't reject it. The House has ceased to be one of latent direction, and has become one of temporary rejectors and palpable alterers.'

As a revising House the vigorous writer from whom I quote maintains the utility of the House of Lords; but, like every other philosophical thinker of recent times, he bases this view upon certain serious defects and vices in the constitution of the House of Commons. It is remarkable that it is impossible to find among the political thinkers in England a defender of the Two House principle on theoretical grounds.

I cannot forbear to make another citation from Mr. Bagehot, who is by no means a Radical or even a Republican, and who, as has been said, maintains the practical utility of the House of Lords.

'There used to be,' he observes, 'a singular idea that two chambers—a revising chamber and a suggesting chamber—were essential to a free government. The first person who threw a hard stone—an effectually hitting stone—against the theory, was one very little likely to be favourable to a democratic influence, or to be blind to the use of aristocracy: it was the present Lord Grey. He had to look at the matter practically. He was the first great colonial minister of England who ever had himself to introduce representative institutions into *all* her capable colonies, and the difficulty stared him in the face that in those colonies there were hardly enough good people for one assembly, and not near enough good people for two assemblies. It happened—and most naturally happened—that a second assembly was mischievous. The second assembly was either the nominee of the Crown, which in such places naturally allied itself with better instructed minds, or was elected by people with a higher property qualification; some peculiarly well-judging people. Both these choosers chose the best men in the colony, and put them into the second assembly.

'And thus the first assembly was necessarily left without these best men. The popular assembly was denuded of those guides and those leaders who would have led and guided it best. Those superior men were put aside to talk to one another, and perhaps dispute with one another: they were a concentrated instance of high but neutralised forces. They wished to do good, but they could do nothing. The Lower House, with all the best people in the colony taken out of it, did what it liked. The democracy was weakened rather than strengthened by the isolation in a weak position of its best opponents. As soon as experience had shown this, or seemed to show it, the theory that two chambers were essential to a good and free government vanished away.'

III.

Having considered the views of the ablest defender of the continued existence of the House of Lords, let us turn to those of one of the many distinguished advocates of the abolition of that House. I quote from Goldwin Smith, late Professor of Modern History in the University of Oxford; the article from which the extract is taken having been written while the author was visiting America and Canada with every opportunity of studying the working of both the one-house and the two-house forms. Professor Smith writes:—

'Not by reason and theory alone, but by overwhelming experience, the House of Lords stands condemned. For three centuries, dating from the Tudor period, it was the most powerful branch of the Legislature, and for a century at least it had, through its nominees and dependents, the virtual control of the other branch. During the whole of that period pressing subjects for legislation abounded, not only in the direction of political reform, but in all directions—legal, ecclesiastical, educational, sanitary, and economical. Yet, in all those centuries, who can point out a single great measure of national improvement which really emanated from the House of Lords? On the other hand, who can point out a single great reform, however urgent at the time, however signally ratified afterwards by the approbation of posterity, which the House of Lords has not thrown out, or obstructed, and, if it could do nothing more, damaged and mutilated to the utmost of its power? As a matter of course, it upheld the rotten boroughs, and resisted the Reform Bill, till it was overcome by the threat of a swamping creation of peers, having first, in its wisdom, brought the nation to the verge of a civil war. As a matter of course, it resisted the progress of religious liberty, because the privileged Church was an outwork of the privileged class. As a matter of course, it resisted, as a noble historian is compelled to confess, the extension of Habeas Corpus and of personal liberty. As a matter of course, it resisted the removal of restraints on the press. As a matter of course, it resisted the introduction of the ballot. All these were measures and movements which threatened political privilege. But the House of Lords has also resisted common measures of humanity, such as the abolition of the Slave Trade, and the reform of Criminal Law. Romilly's Bill for the abolition of the death punishment in cases of petty theft was thrown out by the Lords, and among the thirty-two who voted in the majority on that occasion were seven bishops.

'On all subjects about which popular opinion was not strongly excited, including many of the greatest importance to national progress, Reformers have abstained from moving, because they despaired of overcoming the resistance of the House of Lords. To make legislation on any important question possible, it is necessary to get a storm sufficient to terrify the Peers. *Thus all important legislation is made violent and revolutionary*, and this is your Conservative institution!

'The House of Lords is spoken of as a seat of deliberate wisdom, whose measures undergo maturer consideration than in the less Conservative assembly—a fast nobleman of twenty-one being supposed to be a graver personage than a popular representative at sixty. No popular measures in the House of Lords undergoes any real consideration whatever. Every one of them is condemned before its arrival there—condemned from its very birth: and the discussion in the House of Lords is no discussion, but a mere wavering of the balance between hate and fear. If fear preponderates, the measure lives, and we are called upon to admire the wisdom and tact of the concession. Only oligarchic measures, such as gagging bills and coercion bills, are favoured from their birth, and pass by acclamation.

'Hereditary aristocracy has of late entered on a new phase. As in the Tudor epoch it became an oligarchy of landlordism, now it has become an oligarchy of wealth. The new nobility in this case are the capitalists who, after a temporary antagonism caused by the Corn Laws, and a certain amount of coy resistance on social grounds, have been recognised by the landowners, and in their turn are decking themselves with the titles of feudal barons, ordering Norman pedigrees with their equipages and liveries, doubling the crush and the deliquescence at St. James's, and thinking it a part of their rights as millionaires to make public honour and national government their family property, and to hand them down with the other fruits of successful speculation, to their aristocratically educated sons.

'We are asked what we would put in the place of the House of Lords. Is it necessary to put anything in its place? Is a second Chamber really necessary or desirable? Ontario does very well without one. Quebec is moving to get rid of hers. The Upper Chamber in the Dominion Parliament of Canada is almost a nullity. In Victoria the second Chamber produced a deadlock, which probably would have been repeated in Ontario, if a rivalry of chambers had been added to a rivalry of parties in the constitutional crisis through which the province has just passed. The Upper Chamber is supposed to be a check on unwise legislation. The House of Lords, in a superficial study of which the whole theory of second Chambers seems to have had its source, is a check with a vengeance, because it represents an interest separate from, and adverse to that of the nation. But you cannot really divide the national will. Power will unite somewhere; and it is better to unite with it the full measure of responsibility.

'If the object is to guard against precipitation, that object would be best secured by good legislative forms, and possibly by giving a minority, amounting to a certain proportion of the House, the power of suspending for a certain period the operation of a measure, so as to give time for calmer consideration, and for a possible change of national opinion.'

IV.

The most profound theoretical statement on the subject comes from Mr. John Stuart Mill, who, in his admirable 'Vindication of the French Revolution of 1848, in reply to Lord Brougham and others,' expresses the following opinions:—

'The arguments for a second Chamber, when looked at from one point of view, are of great force, being no other than the irresistible arguments for the necessity or expediency of a principle of antagonism in society—of a counterpoise somewhere to the preponderant power in the State. It seems hardly possible that there should be permanently good government, or enlightened progress, without such a counterpoise. It may, however, be maintained, with considerable appearance of reason, that the antagonism may be more beneficially placed in society itself than in the legislative organ which gives effect to the will of society; that it should have its place in the powers which form public opinion, rather than in that whose proper function is to execute it; that, for example, in a democratic State the desired counterbalance to the impulses and will of the comparatively uninstructed many lies in a strong and independent organisation of the class whose special business is the cultivation of knowledge, and will better embody itself in Universities than in Senates or Houses of Lords.

'A second Chamber, however composed, is a serious hindrance to improvement. Suppose it constituted in the manner, of all others, least calculated to render it an obstructive body; suppose that an Assembly of (say) six hundred persons is elected by universal suffrage, and when elected divides itself, as under the French Directorial Constitution, into two bodies (say) of three hundred each. Now, whereas if the whole body sat as one Chamber, the opposition of three hundred persons, or one-half of the representatives of the people, would be required to throw out an improvement, on the system of separate deliberation one hundred and fifty, or one-fourth only, would suffice. Without doubt, the division into two sections, which would be a hindrance to useful changes, would be a hindrance also to hurtful ones; and the arrangement therefore must be regarded as beneficial by those who think a democratic Assembly is more likely to make hurtful than useful changes. But this opinion both historical and daily experience contradicts.

'There cannot be a case more in point than this very instance in France. The National Assembly was chosen in the crisis of a revolution, by suffrage including all the labouring men of the community; the doctrines of a subversive character which were afloat were peculiarly favourable to the apparent interests of labouring men; yet the Assembly elected was essentially a Conservative body, and it is the general opinion that the legislature now about to be elected will be still more so. The great majority of mankind are, as a general rule, tenacious of things existing; habit and custom predominate with them in almost all cases over remote prospects of advantage; and however popular may be the Constitution in the ordinary course of its working, the difficulty is, not to prevent considerable changes, but to accomplish them when most essentially needful. Any systematic provision in the Constitution to render changes difficult is therefore superfluous—it is injurious.

'It is true, that in the times which accompany or immediately follow a revolution this tendency of the human mind may be temporarily and partially reversed—partially, we say, for a people are as tenacious of old customs and ways of thinking in the crisis of a revolution as at any other time—on all points except those on which they had become strongly excited by a perception of evils or grievances; those, in fact, on which the revolution itself turns. On such points, indeed, there may easily arise, at those periods, an ardour of ill-considered change, and it is at such times, if ever, that the check afforded by a second, or Conservative Chamber might be beneficial. But these are the times when the resistance of such a body is practically null. The very arguments used by the supporters of the institution to make it endurable, assume that it cannot prolong its resistance in excited times. A second Chamber which during a revolution should resolutely oppose itself to the branch of the Legislature more directly representing the excited state of popular feeling, would be infallibly swept away. It is the destiny of a second Chamber to become inoperative in the very cases in which its effective operation would have the best chance of producing less harm than good.'

V.

The above quotations from able English writers form a sufficient commentary upon the statement of the historian of the American Constitution.

It will be seen that the United States has taken up in the supposed interest of liberty that which the best writers on political history in England regard as an impediment to liberty. The question is thus opened, What has been the influence and effect of the two-Chamber system in America?

It is not within my purpose to give here anything like a complete history of the working of the system in America. This is unnecessary, for the character of the system can be illustrated by a reference to the way in which it has worked in the one great emergency which has proved to be the severest test of the strength of Republican institutions in the United States—the Slavery question.

The long and despotic reign of slavery in the Government of the United States culminated in the greatest crime which that country ever committed, namely the unprovoked war upon Mexico. This war was undertaken avowedly for the purpose of obtaining the vast territory of Texas, in order that the area of slavery might be increased and its representation in Congress reinforced. The moral sentiment of the people of the North was outraged by that event and by the deliberate lie under which the President (Polk) and both Houses of Congress combined to shield it. President Polk, in a special Message to Congress, affirmed that 'the Mexicans had at last invaded our territory and shed the blood of our fellow-citizens on our own soil,' and Congress responded by an Act calling out 50,000 volunteers, and appropriating ten millions of dollars to prosecute the struggle, the Act beginning with the words: 'Whereas, by the act of the Republic of Mexico, a state of war exists between that Government and the United States,' &c. The fact that only two Senators and fourteen Representatives dared to vote against this flagrant falsehood was one of the first incidents which brought the American people to a consciousness of the depth of infamy to which the Slave Power had dragged and chained them. Then the thunder tones of Theodore Parker and the electric eloquence of Wendell Phillips began to be listened to, and the keen lash of the author of the 'Biglow Papers' made the descendants of the Puritan Pilgrims writhe under a sense of their degradation.

The crime against Mexico was consummated; but when Slavery came bringing in its blood-stained hands the spoil of which it had robbed

Mexico, and demanded that these conquered territories—in which before the war no slave existed—should now be made over into its own hideous image and likeness, and annexed with that new deformity to the Union, it found a reaction against its tyranny already begun. The reaction manifested itself in the Representative House. That House, the same that had affirmed the lie that war existed by the act of Mexico, now by exactly the same majority — fourteen — passed an Act admitting the territory in question only on condition that slavery should never exist therein.

This Act being sent to the Senate, the latter did not even vote on it, and it fell through.

With this insult the Senate met the first effort of the people through their representatives in the XXIXth Congress, to check the extension of slavery. The XXXth Congress, which gathered in December 1848, indicated that the reaction against the Slave Oligarchy had gained in force. A Bill providing a territorial government for California—part of the vast country seized from Mexico—and prohibiting slavery therein, was passed by a majority of thirty-nine in the House of Representatives.

This Bill having been sent to the Senate, that body refused even to consider it, and it remained dead on the table.

A Bill was brought into the House of Representatives organising a government in Oregon, and prohibiting slavery in that territory. Oregon being farther north than slavery could possibly extend, the champions of that institution made an ingenious effort to reap an advantage by an apparent concession. They agreed to vote for the prohibition of slavery in Oregon, provided this clause were added : ' Inasmuch as the whole of the said territory lies north of thirty-six degrees thirty minutes north latitude, known as the Missouri Compromise.' The object of this addition was to obtain from the House a recognition of the right of Slavery to extend itself in all territory beneath the line named. In other words, Slavery wished to purchase the right to go where it wanted, by conceding the privilege of going where, for physical reasons, it could not go.

This trick did not succeed. The House refused to recognise that Slavery held a mortgage on any part of the national domain, and passed the original Act to organise Oregon, excluding slavery.

The majority was remarkable—ninety-nine! Only thirty-five voted against it, all from Slave States.

The Senate, on the last day of its session, simply laid this Bill on the table, from which it never arose.

In 1849 the House of Representatives passed the usual Appropriation Bill, by which the ways and means of carrying on the machinery of the Government could alone be supplied. The Senate affixed to that necessary Bill a provision that the slaveholders' President should be empowered to extend slavery into the territories and organise them to suit himself. The House of Representatives refused to accept any such amendment. The Senate declared that it would not pass the Appropriation Bill, unless this outrageous claim were conceded, and for a time it seemed that the whole work of the nation would be arrested. This occurred, however, upon the eve of a presidential election which it was necessary for the Slave Power to carry; and fearing to go before the country upon the accusation of having defeated the appropriation of the means necessary for the national machinery, the Senate retreated from this position.

The Upper House now became conscious that

in its effort to enthrone slavery over the whole nation, it had a more difficult task than it had supposed. It had managed to defeat, by its insulting disregard of the measures repeatedly sent up from the popular branch of the Legislature, every effort to organise the territories. It now resolved to try another weapon—bribery.

It happened that there existed in the money market bonds representing the debt of Texas, which were worth from fifteen to twenty per cent. It was known that a large proportion of these bonds were held by members of Congress. In 1850 the Senate passed what were called 'Compromise Measures,' the effect of which was to devote the whole of the territory taken from Mexico, except California, to slavery, and to increase the facilities for catching slaves who should escape from the South, in every part of the Union. It being certain that this Senatorial scheme could not be passed in the Popular House, there was ingeniously slipped into it a provision to pay the State of Texas ten millions, in a stock bearing five per cent. interest, payable out of the United States Treasury, and redeemable at the end of fourteen years. There was absolutely no reason for giving this money to Texas, except the fact that its effect upon the debt of that country, and so upon the bonds held by many Representatives, would make the latter hesitate to defeat the Bill of which it was the bait.

This corrupt scheme succeeded. One House accepted the bribe of the other. The House of Representatives having at first defeated the miserable measure by the weakened majority of eight, re-considered and passed the Act by eleven. So soon as the Act was passed the Texan bonds rose about 85 per cent., and many needy members of Congress suddenly found themselves rich. Mr. Horace Greeley relates that he was told by a Western Governor that he (the Governor) had administered on the estate of one of the Congressmen who helped to pass the Compromise, and found among his assets nearly thirty thousand dollars in Texan bonds, without any indication whatever of how he came by them. As the Congressman had been a man of moderate means, the acquisition of the bonds could be accounted for in but one way.

The Senate—the unbroken bulwark of slavery up to the breaking out of the rebellion—having thus secured for that institution the whole of the south-western territory except California, was less careful about the more northern regions—Nebraska and Kanzas—where the physical features of the country and the climate rendered it impossible that slavery could thrive. Even there, however, it refused to allow any governmental organisation, except on condition that negro bondage should be permissive. This action was the simple abnegation by Congress—the Senate coercing the Lower House by refusing to do anything else—of its duty to provide for the legal settlement of the growing troubles of a territory still held under military control of the President. By that neglect of duty Kanzas was made the arena of civil war. And when, at the end of that war, the free-State men stood victorious, and, in strict conformity with the contract with Congress, passed a Constitution excluding slavery, the Senate refused to admit them into the Union on an anti-slavery basis. They were only able to enter on the day that a large number of the Senators seceded from Congress, and went to their several States to assist in organising a rebellion against the National Union.

During the years covered by this history, the Senate contained the greatest statesmen and the best patriots in America. The most eloquent protests against the throwing of that body across the inevitable path of liberty were uttered there. But these voices, and the steadily rising tide of national feeling against slavery, as manifested in the popular branch of the Legislature, produced hardly any appreciable effect on the Senate, simply because its vote represented a perpetuation of the vice of the first Confederation. The free State, however populous and enlightened, had its vote balanced by the slave State, however thinly settled or ignorant. Delaware was thus the match of New York. Nay, by the purchase of Louisiana, and the annexation of Texas, the balance of power had been thrown on the side of the South, though that section had a free population less than one-fifth in proportion to that of the North.

The fact that along with this moral degradation of the country it had grown in commercial prosperity—a prosperity to which slave-labour had contributed enough to paralyse the consciences of large numbers of Northern people—had led the politicians to continually assert that it was by a certain divine inspiration that the framers of the Constitution had hit upon that exact adjustment of checks and balances whereby freedom and bondage had been enabled so long and so successfully to dwell together in the same Government, and both to grow so rich. This had so long been said that a generation grew up which held to the divine perfections of the American Constitution as a creed. No accusation against a public man or a reformer was so fatal as that he was aiming or willing to touch the Constitution in order to secure his end.

I have already made the humiliating confession that the statesmen of America have not yet challenged the Senate or the Presidency as institutions, because they hope to fill those offices. But I am able to give a more creditable motive for silence concerning the Senate, at least, as having actuated some statesmen in the days when the Upper House was blocking the wheels of the nation. In those days I remember to have asked an eminent Representative in Washington, who bitterly complained that an antiquarian and non-representative body should be able to arrest the will of the country, 'Why, then, do you not strike at the Senate itself, and aim to abolish it?' The Representative smiled at my absurdity, and said, 'It would be the simple ruin of our cause if we admitted that it could not be carried without altering the Constitution. It is a heavy enough burthen to bear that our cause is moral and humane; but to be suspected of placing humanity above the literally infallible Constitution of our Fathers would be death!'

The cause of which this Representative was a champion triumphed at last, only under that power in the Constitution which provides for its own suspension; and that triumph was only rendered secure by the addition of another line to the absolute perfection of that instrument.

There is a tradition that Jefferson coming home from France, called Washington to account at the breakfast-table for having agreed to a second, and, as Jefferson thought, unnecessary legislative Chamber. 'Why,' asked Washington, 'did you just now pour that coffee into your saucer, before drinking?' 'To cool it,' answered Jefferson, 'my throat is not made of brass.' 'Even so,' rejoined Washington, 'we pour our legislation into the senatorial saucer to cool it.' How well the Senate has served the purposes of a cooler may be gathered from the narrative just given of its services during the great emergency in which the energy of every good institution was required. For years it prevented the organisation of the vast territories of the West, because it could not appropriate them to the behests of slavery, by that prevention consigning them to incessant struggles between Indians and irresponsible white settlers, and finally plunging them into terrible civil wars. Kanzas was enabled to gain her place as a free State only by a path stained at every step with the blood of the bravest men, and illuminated by the lurid flames in which the churches, homes, and school-houses of the friends of freedom were consumed. Nay, it was plainly due to the prolonged refusal of the Senate to bend to the determination of two-thirds of the American people to arrest the further expansion of slavery, that the possibility of settling the issue between the North and South by any peaceful formulas was at last made apparent, and the fearful Civil War, in which slavery perished, became a dire necessity. So much for the Cooler!

VI.

Hitherto I have spoken only of the Upper House, that whose constitution makes it a plain anomaly in a Republican country, and whose history recalls the worst obstructions placed in the path of English liberty by the House of Peers, which it avowedly copied. I now turn to consider the defects of the House of Representatives which are directly traceable to the existence of two Chambers.

It is already on record that in the most critical moment of the national history the Popular House had its balance of power turned away from the support of freedom by a pecuniary bribe, and gave its voice in favour of the infamous measures demanded by slavery. This corruption has not been frequent in the Congressional history of the United States, but so salient a proof of its possibility would not blot the escutcheon of the Republic, had that House represented the best elements of the nation which elected it. It has often been stated in Monarchical countries, as a charge against Republican institutions, that the best thinkers in America avoid politics and refuse office. The statement is exaggerated, and in its general scope unfounded. Men of culture and ability, even men of letters, in America participate in politics as earnestly as the same classes do in other countries. But so far as the statement concerns the House of Representatives, it is but too well grounded. That House has never been an object of ambition to the most eminent American thinkers, who have much preferred—like Motley, Bancroft, Marsh, Jay, and others—to serve their country in other capacities.

The Popular House gained the reputation of being hardly a fit place for a gentleman during the long reign of slavery; the Southern members in it having more confidence in the bowie knife and the bludgeon, which they were accustomed to wield so effectively on the cotton plantation, than in argument. But though their departure from it at the period of Secession left it a more orderly body, the House has never risen to the level of the intelligence or character of the nation, and its deficiencies have been proved to have a much deeper root than the temporary domination of the slaveholders. Admitting all that may be claimed for the talent that is in it—remembering, as every American must, the high principle and the force of some of its members—it is impossible at this moment to assert that it contains a man of commanding power or of general reputation. Hardly one name in that body can be written down here which would not be entirely new to every European reader. The names of its veterans, its best and noblest men, call up honourable associations in the minds of Americans, but almost none at all to people in foreign lands; and it must be admitted that the Representative Assembly of the greatest Republic in the world has acquired but little reputation for ability beyond its own walls.

This charge might not weigh so heavily if it had, as a body, commanded the confidence of the friends of freedom throughout the world. But it would be difficult to point to an instance in which any eminent European Liberal or Radical has pointed with pride to the American House of Representatives. Have Mill, Mazzini, Louis Blanc, Karl Blind, ever pointed their advocacy of popular institutions with confident allusions to the greatness of the Chamber which chiefly represents them in America? Nay, have writers and orators in the United States found there illustrations of the greatness of their country's Constitution?

Besides the lack of general culture or signal ability in that House, it has notoriously shown a tendency toward hasty legislation. I need only point to the eagerness and ostentation with which it welcomed Commodore Wilkes when he came with the Confederate envoys illegally captured from an English ship, and approved his act, preparing thus for the nation an unnecessarily humiliating retreat from an untenable position. Witness also the insulting resolutions which the House passed concerning England during the Alabama controversy—resolutions which might have caused war between the two countries had the body which passed them possessed sufficient weight in America to have carried public support. The resolutions were so little noticed in America that they were hardly commented on in England. But I need not multiply examples. The House of Representatives has abroad a worse reputation than it merits, for much of its odour lingers from the Southern 'fire-eaters' who so long raged in it; but its inferior position in the eyes of the world, in comparison with the eminence of the United States, requires no demonstration.

It is impossible to trace this inferiority to any other cause than the fact that it is, and feels itself to be, only a half-Legislature. The Senate having been established by tradition of the House of Lords, though it is only of equal power theoretically with the Lower House, has a conventional superiority of rank awarded it. Nay, even in its constitution it has certain elements of superiority, particularly in its preponderant share in the disposal of Foreign Affairs, the confirmation of ambassadors, and in its special relation, as an advisory body, with the President. Moreover, the Senators are required to be older men than the Representatives. It has thus become the tradition of the country that it is out of the Senate that the chief officers of the nation are to be chosen. A presidential candidate, or a judge for the Supreme Bench, is pretty regularly selected from among the Senators. By this means the Senate has become the stepping-stone to the higher official positions, and, by consequence, the House of Representatives has been reduced to a training-school for the Senate. It is probable that there is not a Representative who is not aiming to become a Senator; certainly not one who would not eagerly leave the 'Lower' for the 'Higher' branch. The result of this, is that a depletion of ability and mature wisdom from the House of Representatives is perpetually going on. Statesmen in England have been known to deplore their necessary transfer from the House of Commons to the House of Peers; but an instance where an American Representative has been unwilling to abandon the Popular for the Senatorial body is unknown. No sooner has an individual in that House shown distinguished ability than he manages to secure promotion to the Upper House, the result being somewhat as if Mr. Gladstone and Mr. Disraeli, and all their leading followers, should be taken away from the House of Commons, leaving legislation there to—Heaven knows whom! For this reason alone the House of Representatives in America can never have a permanent character of its own, can never attract the ambition of the ablest men for itself, and can never command the confidence of the United States or of the world.

But, apart from the question of social and political rank, the merely preliminary character of the legislation in either of the two Houses has been unquestionably reflected in the hasty action which has been repeatedly observed in the lower branch of Congress. It was but natural that this haste should be more characteristic of the Lower House, because of its more youthful composition, and of the higher social rank of the Senate already alluded to. The Senate has not, indeed, been free from the fault of legislating sometimes in deliberate defiance of the Lower House, and rather to snub the inferior body than to enact its own will.

Some of the most eminent Senators have been known to express publicly their contempt of the House of Representatives. Soon after Mr. Douglas had been transferred from the House to the Senate, he made a motion to forward some Bill, when Daniel Webster, the famous Senator from Massachusetts, said, without rising from his seat, 'We have no such practice in the Senate, sir!' Mr. Douglas having soon after endeavoured to forward his measure in another way, Mr. Webster said more sternly, 'That is not the way we do business in the Senate, sir!' The anecdote not only recalls the contempt with which the House was regarded by the Senators only twenty years ago, but it may remind any one who was in the habit of attending Congressional debates in those years, as was the case of the present writer, that the contempt was not altogether unmerited, though the right of the Senate to feel it might be well doubted.

VII.

Perhaps no truer picture can be given of the manner in which business was conducted in the House before the rebellion—its manners and procedure have much improved since—than in Mr. Horace Greeley's reminiscences of his experience as a member of it. Mr. Greeley was elected to represent a district of New York City, and took his seat in 1848. He sat during one term with Abraham Lincoln; and it is, in my opinion, far less to the discredit of these two able and honest friends of liberty than to the character of the House that they sat in it almost as silent members. The extracts I subjoin from Mr. Greeley's 'Recollections of a Busy Life,' were written without the remotest reference to the subject which we are considering, but they bear upon it in a way that cannot be mistaken.

'Abraham Lincoln,' writes Mr. Greeley, 'and Andrew Johnson (each of them then about forty years old) were members of the House to which I was chosen, as Mr. Johnson had been of the two preceding and remained through the two following, when he was translated to the Senate. Mr. Johnson, being a Democrat, seldom visited our side of the hall, and I saw much less of him than of Mr. Lincoln, who was a Whig, and who, though a new member, was personally a favourite on our side. He seemed a quiet, good-natured man, did not aspire to leadership, and seldom claimed the floor. I think he made but one set speech during that session, and this speech was by no means a long one. Though a strong partisan, he voted against the bulk of his party once or twice, when that course was dictated by his convictions. He was one of the most moderate, though firm, opponents of slavery extension, and notably of a buoyant, cheerful spirit.'

'Sundry attempts at reforming what were considered abuses were made that winter, but without brilliant success. We tried to abolish flogging in the navy, but were beaten. I think it was Mr. (now General) Schenck who raised a laugh against us by proposing so to amend that the commander of a ship of war should never order a sail spread or reefed without calling out all hands and taking a vote of his crew on the question. We were temporarily successful in voting in committee to stop dealing out strong drink to the sailors and marines in our navy, though this, too, was ultimately defeated; but, in the first flush of our delusive triumph, a member sitting near me, who had voted to stop the grog ration, said to a friend who, I believe, had voted the same way, " Gid, that was a glorious vote we have just taken." " Yes, glorious," was the ready response. " Gid," resumed the elated reformer, " let us go and take a drink on the strength of it." " Agreed," was the willing echo; and they went.'

' An abuse had crept in, a few years before, at the close of a long exhausting session, when some liberal soul had proposed that each of the sub-officers and attachés of Congress (whose name is legion) be paid two hundred and fifty dollars extra because of such protracted labour. Thenceforth, this gratuity was repeated at the close of each session; the money being taken by the generous members, not out of their own pockets, but Uncle

Sam's, and the vote being now that "the *usual* extra compensation" &c. As our session was a light as well as a short one, some of us determined to stop this Treasury leak; and we did it once or twice, to the chagrin of the movers. At length came the last night of the session, and with it a magnificent "spread," free to all members, in one of the committee-rooms, paid for by a levy of five dollars per head from the regiment of underlings who hoped to thus secure their "usual" gratuity; giving each a net profit on the investment of two hundred and forty-five dollars. After the House had been duly mellowed and warmed, a resolve to pay the "usual extra compensation" was sprung, but failed—two-thirds in the affirmative being necessary to effect the requisite suspension of the rules. Nothing daunted, the operators drew off to repair damages; and soon there was moved a resolve to pay the chaplain of the House his stipend from the Contingent Fund, and to suspend the rules, to accord this resolve an immediate consideration.

'" I object, Mr. Speaker," I at once interposed; "we all know that the chaplain's salary has not been left unprovided for to this time. This is a *ruse*.

I call for the Yeas and Nays on suspending the rules."

'"Shame! shame!" rose and reverberated on every side. "Don't keep the chaplain out of his hard-earned money! Refuse the Yeas and Nays!"

'They were accordingly refused; the rules were indignantly suspended, and the resolution received.

'"And now, Mr. Speaker," said the member who had been cast for this part, "I move to amend the resolve before us by adding the usual extra commission to the sub-clerks, door-keepers, and other *employés* of the House."

'No sooner said than done: debate was cut off, and the amendment prevailed. The resolve, as amended, was rushed through; and our *employés* pocketed their two hundred and fifty dollars each, less the five dollars so recently and judiciously invested as aforesaid.'

'I was placed by the Speaker on the Committee on Public Lands, whereof Judge Collamer, of Vermont, was Chairman, and which was mainly composed of worthy, upright men, intent on standing up for public right against private greed.

'Various fair-seeming Bills and claims came before us, some of which had passed the Senate, yet which we put our heel on as barefaced robberies. At length there came along a meek, innocent-looking stranger, by whom we were nicely taken in and thoroughly done for. It was a Bill to cede to the several New States (so-called) such portions of the unsold public lands within their limits respectively as were submerged or sodden, and thus rendered useless and pestilential; that is, swamps, marshes, bogs, fens, &c. These lands, we were told, were not merely worthless while undrained, they bred fevers, ague, and all manner of zymotic diseases, shortening the lives of pioneers, and rendering good lands adjacent unhealthy and worthless. But cede these swamp lands to the States including them respectively, on condition that they should sell them and devote the proceeds to draining and improving them, and everything would be lovely; the neighbouring dry lands would sell readily, and the Treasury be generously replenished. There was never a cat rolled whiter in meal, and I, for one, was completely duped. As I recollect, the Bill did not pass that session; but we reported strongly in its favour, and that report, doubtless, aided to carry the measure through the next Congress. The consequence was, a reckless and fraudulent transfer to certain States of millions on millions of choice public lands, whole sections of which had not muck enough on their surface to accommodate a fair-sized frog, while the appropriation of the proceeds to draining proved a farce and a sham. The lands went, all of them that had standing water enough on a square mile of their surface to float a duck in March, with a good deal more beside, while never a shake or an ague has any pioneer been spared by reason of all the drainage done under this precious Act.'

'The last night of a session is usually a long one, and ours was not only long, but excited. The two Houses were at variance; the House desiring (at least voting) to prohibit the introduction of slavery into the vast territories just then acquired from Mexico, the Senate dissenting from that policy. Of course, we who voted for the restriction could not carry it through nor over the Senate. But that body was not content to stand on the defensive: it attached to the great Civil and Diplomatic Appropriation Bill (since divided) a provision for the organisation of the new territories—of course without the restriction against slavery—and, in effect, said to us, "You shall agree to this, or the new (Taylor) Administration shall not have a dollar to spend after the 1st of July ensuing." We had one or two conferences by committee, but neither House would give way. Finally the Bill came back to us on this last evening, the Senate insisting on its territorial amendment. Each side had rallied its full force (there were but three of all the Representatives chosen from the Slave States who were not in their seats), and we were morally certain to be beaten on a motion to recede, three or four weak brethren changing their votes rather than leave the Government penniless, when some one on our side got in a motion to *concur with an amendment.* This amendment accepted the Senate's project of organising the new territories, barely adding a stipulation that *the existing laws thereof should remain in force till changed by consent of Congress.* (The existing laws were those of Mexico, and forbade slavery.) This motion prevailed (as I recollect, the vote on one important division stood one hundred and eleven to one hundred and ten), and completely changed the whole aspect of the matter. The pro-slavery men were now as anxious to expunge the territorial clause as they had previously been determined to insert it at all hazards; and the Senate struck out its cherished provision, and let the Appropriation Bill pass as it originally was, leaving the question of slavery in the new territory as a legacy of trouble to the incoming Administration. Never was a parliamentary move more clever than that motion to concur with an amendment.

'When it had been carried through our House, and while the Senate was chewing upon it, there ensued a hiatus, or interregnum—the House having really nothing to do but wait. At such times any member who has a pet project or Bill asks a suspension of the rules in favour of its consideration. Among these motions was one by Mr. Robert W. Johnson, of Arkanzas, who wished the House to consider a Bill providing payment for horses lost by his constituents while acting as volunteers in Indian wars. His motion to suspend the rules failed; when I drew from my drawer a resolve, which had lain there for weeks, proposing that our country take the general name of COLUMBIA, in honour of the great discoverer. I was making a few remarks introductory to my motion to suspend the rules—which I knew would be defeated—when Mr. R. W. Johnson turned upon Mr. O. B. Ficklin, of Illinois, who sat very near him, and angrily said, "Ficklin, why do you always oppose any motion I make?" "I did not oppose your motion," was the prompt and true reply. "You lie!" rejoined Johnson, whose powers of observation were not then in their best estate, and he sprang forward as though to clutch Ficklin, when Mr. Samuel W. Inge, of Alabama, rushed upon the latter, and struck him two or three blows with a cane. "Order, order!—Serjeant-at-Arms, do your duty!" interposed the Speaker; and the affray was promptly arrested. "Why, Inge, what did you fall upon Ficklin for?" enquired one of his neighbours; Ficklin being an intensely pro-slavery Democrat, as were Inge and Johnson. "Why, I thought," explained Inge, "that the fight between the North and the South had commenced, and I might as well pitch in." I did not hear him say this, but it was reported to me directly afterwards, and I have no doubt that he said and thought so.

'Mr. Giddings went over to the Democratic side of the House that night, and made some jocular remark to an acquaintance on the change of aspect since we had made and sustained our motion to concur with an amendment, when he was assailed, and was glad to get away quite rapidly. I am confident I could not have passed quietly through that side of the House between ten and two o'clock of that night without being assaulted, and, had I resisted, beaten within an inch of my life, if not killed outright. Yet I had proposed nothing, said nothing, on the exciting topic; I was obnoxious only because I was presumed earnestly hostile to slavery.'

It is true that the ruffianism which used to flourish in the House up to the breaking out of the Civil War ceased when the Southerners left Congress to take part in the rebellion. The corruption by which fraudulent Bills are passed is perhaps the most serious charge against that body. It is a sad indication of the kind of men who constituted it twenty-five years ago, that they could permit its subordinates to prepare a banquet in one of its Congressional committee-rooms, and that members could, by an appeal to their palates, be induced to pass a fraudulent measure for the advantage of those functionaries, not to speak of other and worse things.

recorded by Mr. Greeley. It would be a satisfaction to learn from the same writer, than whom a more capable and honest observer of public affairs does not exist in America, that the House had gained in honesty as well as in decorum since purged of its more violent spirits. But on this point we have from him the following testimony, with which I conclude these extracts.

'I do not imply that legislation, whether in Congress or elsewhere, is purer and cleaner now than it was twenty or forty years ago. On the contrary, I judge that it is oftener swayed, to the prejudice of the public interest, by considerations of personal advantage, and that the evil tends strongly to increase and diffuse itself. The chartering of railroads through public lands which are required (as is clearly just) to contribute to their construction, whether by liberal grants of territory or by direct subsidies in cash, and many kindred devices for promoting at once public and private prosperity, have strongly tended to render legislation mercenary, whether in Congress, in State Legislatures, or in Municipal Councils. When I was in the House, there were ten or twelve members—not more than twelve I am confident—who were generally presumed to be "on the make," as the phrase is; and they were a class by themselves, as clearly as if they were so many black sheep in a large flock of white ones. I would gladly believe that this class has not since increased in numbers or in impudence; but the facts do not justify that presumption.'

VIII.

The facts stated warrant the conclusion that where there are two Houses of Legislature the following results may be expected.

1. There will be a continual rivalry between the Houses. This will introduce into their dealings with each other something of the spirit of the cockpit. The *esprit de corps*, which in a single House enables parties to base their antagonism solely on principles, and to dismiss all personal influences which can only weigh in debate to the public detriment, is intensified and made into an habitual element in legislation where it is divided. In England this influence is repeatedly seen at work with most undesirable results. Whatever arguments the Lords may urge against a Bill sent

to them by the Commons, the latter, if only for the sake of pluck, must insist upon their Bill, or something sufficiently like it to give the Upper House the appearance of having yielded. In addition to the advantages of the Commons' measure must be considered the necessity that the Lords must always give way to the representative body, right or wrong. In the United States the theoretical equality of the two Chambers stimulates each to this self-assertion in matters where any obtrusion of the selfhood of an assembly is more injurious, if less impertinent, than the personality of an individual.

2. In the course of this rivalry one of the estates represented will be proved to be the stronger, and the legislative Chamber representing it will assume a position of superiority. It will then gradually acquire powers not originally assigned to it by an accumulation of special enactments. It was by this means that the House of Lords became a Supreme Court. The House of Commons, having in turn become the more powerful, similarly added to its powers. The written Constitution of America has, indeed, prevented such technical increase or modification of the legal

power of either House of Congress, but it has not availed to prevent the assumption by Senators of many of the airs of an aristocracy, and their gradual acquisition of a preponderant influence in legislation.

3. As a consequence of the gradual accumulation of power in the House that proves to be the stronger there will ensue a deterioration in the composition of the inferior House. Able and eminent men will decline to become candidates for it, or if they are chosen to it will only use it as a stepping-stone to the higher branch, and thus the Lower House will be made over to a combination of young aspirants, immature politicians, and those who have not sufficient ability or character to pass to the higher position.

4. The incompetency of a Chamber to which the stream of immaturity is continually flowing, and from which the best elements are continually ebbing, will be reinforced by the constant presence of the feeling that it is, at best, only half-legislating. Ordinary measures—which often prove to have consequences of greater importance than those which excite strong partisan antagonisms—will be more hastily brought forward and more in-

considerately passed, when each member feels that he is merely voting for something that may or may not become law. The average indolence is invited to throw upon the other Chamber of Congress the onus of more seriously considering and adequately moulding the measure which a single House can only set in motion. And as the other House legislates under a similar knowledge that its work is to be revised, it is very doubtful whether in either House a measure is pondered by men impressed by the sense of full responsibility, or by such solemn feeling as would be inspired by the knowledge that their action passes at once to be the law of the land. During some years' residence in Washington I frequently witnessed instances of what seemed to me almost frivolous legislation, which I am confident could not have occurred had there been a single House of Congress. The very same men who, on some imposing question which had brought on a conflict between the two Houses, could be defiant and resist the rival House in the spirit of the prize-ring, simply because it was another House, would on some less agitating occasion lazily throw the larger part of their duty upon the other body.

5. If two Houses of Legislature are established, it is necessary that they shall have different bases. There can be manifestly no advantage, but only needless cumbrousness, in having two Chambers representing the same constituent elements. The two Chambers of the State Legislatures, for example, are thus composed. One House represents the townships, corresponding to English boroughs; the other represents the counties, or groups of counties, arranged on the basis of population. Both, therefore, are popular bodies, the only difference being in their size. The result is, that the thirty-seven States are cumbered, for the most part, with thirty-seven expensive nullities. Where the second Chamber of the State Legislature aspires to be more than the proverbial fifth wheel to a coach, it only adds another field for the play of lobbyism and corruption, or it produces dead locks like those which, as we have seen, have impeded the work of the Australian Legislatures. And when these dead-locks occur, they have to be settled by a conference of the two Houses; that is, by the more effectual method of the Legislators temporarily constituting themselves into a single Chamber. The representation of the people and the

aristocracy in England, and the representation of the States and of the people in America, need not, indeed, have been shaped in two parliamentary branches, but the arrangement is not so absurd as it would be, for example, in France, where, in order to establish a second legislative branch, some new basis would have to be invented, or some new order created, in order that the new Chamber might have something to represent. If different social or political orders exist in a country, even those who would not regard such difference of interests as a misfortune would admit, that they might easily become so by being sharply defined, sundered in counsels, and placed under different flags. All will admit that if different ranks, orders, or class-interests exist, there is the utmost necessity that they should be represented in a form where they may meet face to face in loyalty to some common tribunal, so that personal harmony at least may be preserved, even if political antagonism must for a time remain. But when such several representatives do not meet face to face, when they sit in different bodies, each with its own *amour propre*, the interests or orders in question are really pitted against each other, and every dividing force—however little related to the real differences of interest—is brought into the conditions of perpetual exasperation. For many years legislation in America was but an exchange of insults between the two Houses of Congress. These were a clear and needless addition to the affronts given and received between opposing parties in each House. The jealousy between the the States-Rights element and the Popular principle was simply intensified by their being potted off, so to say, into two jars, which were perpetually snapping at each other. The positive and negative forces would, indeed, have been equally definite if they had both been in one jar, but the snapping would have ceased, and the two poles might have been able to co-operate even by reason of their antagonism. As it is, the separation into two Houses of Congress of the two jarring interests which the Constitution had compromised, served to keep alive differences that otherwise might have vanished, and to preserve in a state of perpetual irritation and self-assertion principles that might have converged had their representatives sat side by side, and met face to face in debate. The experience of America has certainly shown that a national Union is naturally reflected in unity of legislation.

IX.

In conclusion of this part of my subject, I will simply refer to the only argument used in favour of the principle of two Houses which seems to me to have the least weight. It is said that majorities may be oppressive, and that there ought to be some means of checking their absolute dominion. This is certainly true; and to do this without making that check prevail only to delay a measure until it is too late to be of benefit, or to take from a measure so much as is disagreeable to one class, leaving its other defects untouched, or to pass a measure in form with the pith abstracted —the method in England and America—is the most important political problem of our time. Whatever may be the right plan, history has demonstrated the falsity of the Two-House method.

There exists in the Constitution of the United States a feature which has been somewhat veiled under the over-ready assertion of the presidential prerogative of the Veto, but which, I believe, points in the direction from which the just check to the possible tyranny of a legislative majority is to come. I allude to the authority of the Supreme Court to annul decisions of Congress which are contrary to the Constitution, or to its spirit. The earnest discussion which occurred in the Convention which framed the American Constitution as to whether this final power should be lodged in the Supreme Court proves that its importance was felt. It now stands that though both Houses of Congress may have passed an Act, and the President may have signed it, any individual who deems himself thereby wronged, may appeal to the Supreme Court, and that Court may decide whether the Act is constitutional, and if it be not may annul it. The experience of the United States has indeed shown the necessity that such a Court should be constituted with extreme caution, and placed much further beyond the control of partisan influences than is the case in that country. To leave the appointment of judges to a President has been found to result in the promotion of partisans to that high position; and the lack of any provision against the nomination of any member of it to the Presidency or other office which may be thought higher, has left that bench open to temptations against which its occupants have not been proof. But even with these defects the Supreme Judiciary in the United States has demonstrated that, with just precautions of the kind indicated, it might be made into an ultimate tribunal which would preserve the rights of every citizen and community, and command the confidence of the entire country. Proceedings in this Court might be made easier by a provision that where, in the opinion of one or more of the judges, any case has a *prima facie* right to be heard, the promoter shall be relieved from the costs of a trial, whatever the result. If this judicial power to check hasty or tyrannical legislation were supplemented by the power of a Prime Minister and his Cabinet to return a measure to the Legislature with objections, and demand a slightly increased majority for its final enactment; and if, further, in case a measure so returned were re-enacted, and it were deemed of sufficient importance, there were reserved to the Executive the right to appeal to the suffrages of the nation upon it, the dangers from partisan majorities would be reduced so far as they can safely be under the present régime of representative government.

But the desirable end can only be absolutely

attained when, in addition to the partial negative of the Executive to secure reconsideration, and the ultimate authority of a disinterested Judiciary, the Republic shall secure for each respectable minority the proportionate degree of representation to which its numerical strength or its ability may entitle it. I cannot here go into the discussion of the subject on the representation of minorities; but I cannot wonder that some able men in England, Professor Fawcett among others, should base their only hesitation in advocating the immediate abolition of the House of Lords upon the unsatisfactory composition of the House of Commons as regards minorities. Nevertheless, experience has shown that the improvement of the House of Commons has proceeded in a direct ratio with a reduction of the power of the House of Lords, and there is reason to believe that the entire lopping off the hereditary branch would be speedily followed by the concentration of all the living energies of the country in the remaining Chamber to an extent which would make it in reality what it now pretentiously claims to be—the first legislative assembly in the world.

THE PRESIDENT.

I.

I LATELY met in London Charles Sumner, the veteran of the United States Senate, and truest statesman in America—a man in whose eloquence and fidelity are reflected, for the living generation, the patriotism and the courage which achieved the independence, and furnished the equal laws of their country.

When I had last seen Senator Sumner it was as he lay on his bed, struck down by an assassin's blow, because he had raised his voice against the despot of his country—Slavery. When I saw him just now in London, it was with the old trouble that resulted from that assault returning upon him, compelling him to seek again the medical skill of France; a trouble that had been revived by the long and bitter persecution he had endured from another despotic power—the President of the United States.

General Ulysses Grant, the lucky commander into whose hand the leader of the exhausted Southern Confederacy surrendered his sword, was made President as the symbol of victory. From claiming the credit of having saved the country, it was with him an easy step to imagine that the country belonged to him. Certainly, never did any President—which is saying much—devote his official position so freely to private ends. Against all the traditions of the nation, he accepted personal gifts from wealthy men, accepted a fine summer residence, coach and horses, and even a large sum of money, and in return, offered office to those who gave these gifts. He appointed nearly forty of his relatives and connections to lucrative offices, the individuals so appointed being ignorant persons entirely without claim to the positions awarded them. The nation was disgusted at this disregard of its traditions, and recurrence to the nepotism by which so many Governments have been corrupted, but, nevertheless, the President was able to obtain from the Senate confirmations of his appointments, and received no public reprobation for his offences.

An adventurer who had usurped power in St. Domingo, being unable to sustain himself, resolved on the desperate expedient of making over that island to the United States, as consideration for its furnishing protection to his failing dynasty. The proposition did credit to the astuteness of the negro race. The pretender, Baez, and his dependents saw in the presidential chair at Washington, a man whose singleness of devotion to his own interest had stimulated an otherwise commonplace mind to a certain ingenuity. They saw this President already laying his plans to add another term of four years to an official existence whose good fame was strictly limited to those enjoying its patronage. They knew also that the only form in which any Mephistopheles could successfully assail the average American, was by taking him into a high mountain and offering him an extension of territory; and that if, when the verdict upon his conduct was to be given, the President could point to an enlargement of the national domain during his administration, a multitude of sins would be forgotten in the glory of the new star added to the flag.

Never did one intriguer more accurately divine the mind of another than when Baez of Domingo offered that island to Grant of Washington. The President at once urged the annexation upon Congress, when, lo! to his astonishment, the Senate hesitated. Emboldened by a remembrance of the previous servilities of that body in the confirmation of his many wretched appointments, the President proceeded to use secret bribes and open threats to carry his end.

He might have succeeded, had he not lost his head. For a generation it had been observed that no regularly elected President had ever set his heart upon a measure but he managed to carry it through Congress. President Grant, enraged that the first serious resistance to the executive control over legislation should have occurred in his case, resolved to fight his opponents desperately. But in his fury he delivered a blind stroke which fell upon himself. He despatched ironclads to give military protection to Baez against that pretender's opponents, without any permission from Congress; whereas of all the powers assigned to the National Legislature by the Constitution, none is more jealously reserved thereto than every movement having the slightest relation to war. The sword of the nation can in no conceivable case stir from its scabbard save at the solemn demand of Congress. The President of the United States by this plain violation of the Constitution, gave just enough reinforcement to his opponents to enable them to defeat his designs on Domingo, and to raise the extraordinary landmark which declares to the astonished Republic, 'Here the mandate of a President to Congress was successfully resisted.' The burthen of this conflict—the most significant in the history of the United States within this century—fell upon Charles Sumner, Senator of Freedom's pioneer State, Massachusetts. Upon him the President wreaked his utmost vengeance. He secured, through his tools in the Senate, the degradation of that Senator from the important Committee of which he had been for many years the able chairman. Mr. Motley, the eminent historian, was removed from his position as Minister to England, without warning, and before he had fairly entered upon his office, simply because he was believed to be a friend of Mr. Sumner, at whose request he was supposed to have been appointed. The Senator of Massachusetts triumphed only at the cost of dividing the Republican party which he had previously led, and to the detriment of his physical health.

It was under these circumstances that he had been compelled to abandon all hope of participation in the critical Presidential struggle of 1872. The President, unable to come before the people claiming re-election on his merits either as an administrator in his own, or a successful grabber of his neighbour's territory, had bluntly fallen back upon his real strength. That is, he had turned the whole machinery of Government to the one purpose of his own re-election. Every office-holder under him, from the Cabinet Minister to the smallest postmaster in the nation, was for several months consecrated to this end alone. When the time approached for the nomination of a Republican candidate for the Presidency, the independent adherents of that party—those who had held no office under Grant—protested vehemently that they would not have this man for another four years. Since the foundation of the Government there had not been so general or so earnest a disgust expressed towards the President by the very men who had raised him to power. The thinkers, the scholars, the anti-slavery men, all expressed earnest dissatisfaction at the utter selfishness and ignorance which had characterised his administration.

The President vouchsafed no reply. He recalled none of his stupid relatives whom he had appointed to high positions. He promised no amendment for the future. He simply snapped his fingers in the faces of the malcontents, who represented the intelligence and character of the country. He knew that he had behind him a hundred thousand office-holders in and out of the country whose official heads might fall with his, and was in a position to dictate his nomination to the Republican party. The nominating Convention met and cast their votes for him with a predestined and machine-like unanimity. They could not help themselves.

The disgusted and dissatisfied members of the party made a tremendous effort to break this chain, and gathered in Cincinnati, by their delegates, to nominate an opponent. They selected a man of character, of life-long fidelity to every interest of the country and of humanity, and of literary eminence; but from the first this opposition was fighting a lost cause. The power which had forced upon the main body of the strongest party the re-nomination of the existing President was felt to be able to force him equally upon the people.

For some months the people of the United States have seen the whole official power of the country turned to the one purpose of securing a new lease of office to an individual. They have witnessed the hitherto unknown sight of the President's Cabinet Ministers abandoning entirely their posts of duty at Washington, and taking the stump through the country for Grant. They have seen every office-holder, even female clerks, systematically taxed for the election-expenses of their chief. They have seen the national post-office converted into a great engine for scattering through the nation franked laudations of Grant, and slanders of his opponents. And as the result of this they have seen the most unpopular President known in the country's history (of those chosen by the people) re-elected by an enormous majority. And it is well enough that it should be so. Any other result would misrepresent the condition of the country. It is but fair that America should confess, and that the world should know, that the presidential power, concentrated upon the interest of its possessor, is irresistible.

It has been necessary that I should enter into these details, for they were all immediately behind the veteran Senator whom I met in London, and gave weight to his words.

II.

'We have,' said the Senator, 'arrived at a period in our national history when the personal power of the President is almost irresistible. For many years the powers of checking his will in Congress have been becoming weaker and weaker, until a single act of resistance now requires every sinew and every nerve which the nation can bring to bear through its representatives. The evil has gone on until the Chief Magistrate has come to regard constitutional opposition to any scheme of his own in the light of a rebellion or a crime which the Executive must punish. This is at present, in my opinion, our most serious national danger. We fairly parallel the condition of things which existed in Great Britain nearly a century ago, when the House of Commons adopted a resolution declaring "that the influence of the Crown has increased, is increasing, and ought to be diminished." The military spirit fostered by the late war, and increased by the election of General Grant, has brought this formidable tendency to its climax. If Grant be re-elected, no one can contend that it is because he is regarded by the American people as the worthiest citizen to be their Head. It will be due entirely to the army of office-holders, representing a complete organisation of drilled and interested persons, who, having forced him on the country as a candidate, are devoting the whole resources of the Government, and a power of patronage not possessed by any other monarch in the world, to the one purpose of his re-election.'

'What remedy is there for this?'

The Senator shakes his head.

'It is a long work—longer, I fear, than our people are aware of. The absolute power of one man over the Civil Service of the country, by which many of the most prominent persons in every community are by their interests placed directly under his control, is implicated; but the first step open to us at present seems to be unquestionably the limitation of every President to a single term of office. That, at least, would prevent his using his enormous patronage for the purpose of prolonging his power.'

'But is it not just possible,' I urge, 'not to say

probable, that if an ambitious or selfish President were unable to use his power and patronage to secure his own re-election, he might still find some personal advantage to which he might devote it? It might be a pecuniary advantage with one; it might be with another the election of some favourite to be his successor—some relative, perhaps his eldest son!'

The Senator was fully alive to the dangers of an Hereditary Presidency, and knew well that the practical measures he had suggested were but palliatives. There is no man living who less needs instruction as to the depth of the peril to save the nation from which he has devoted his life. And when I at length put it to him plainly whether he did not think things might have been better had the authors of the Constitution, as at one time it seemed probable they would, instituted an Executive Commission instead of the Presidency, he replied with earnestness that such a modification of the Constitution had repeatedly occurred to him, and that it was by no means certain that the Republic would not be compelled to preserve itself by the total destruction of the One-Man Power.

III.

To this testimony of the most distinguished American Senator may be fitly added the reasoning of the most eminent political thinker in England. Mr. John Stuart Mill, in his Vindication of the French Republicans of 1848, against Lord Brougham and other critics, made the following remarks on the subject of the Presidency, which, in the light of events which have since occurred, add to their weight of argument the impressiveness of fulfilled prophecy.

'We dissent altogether,' wrote Mr. Mill, 'from the common opinion of democratic Republicans, which tends to multiply the conferring of offices by popular election. The sovereign Assembly, which is the organ of the people for superintending and controlling the Government, must of necessity be so elected. But, with this exception, it appears to us certain (what even Bentham, though in his earlier speculations he maintained a different opinion, ultimately acknowledged) that judges, administrators, functionaries of all sorts, will be selected with a much more careful eye to their qualifications, if some conspicuous public officer, a President or a Minister, has the choice of them imposed on him as part of his peculiar business, and feels his official character and the tenure of his own power to depend, not on what the people may now think of the choice made, but on what they will think of it after trial. It seems equally certain that the President or Prime Minister will be better selected by the people's representatives than by the people themselves directly. The example of the United States is a strong argument for this opinion. If the President were elected by Congress, he would generally be the leader and acknowledged ablest man of his party. Elected by the people, he is now always either an unknown mediocrity, or a man whose reputation has been acquired in some other field than that of politics. Nor is this likely to alter, for every politician who has attained eminence has made a multitude of at least political enemies, which renders him a less available candidate for his party to put forward than somebody of the same professed principles who is comparatively obscure.

'It is to be feared that the appointment of a President by the direct suffrages of the community will prove to be the most serious mistake which the framers of the French Constitution have made. They have introduced by it into the still more fermentable elements of French society what even in America is felt to be so great an evil—the turmoil of a perpetual canvass, and the baneful habit of making the decision of all great public questions depend less upon their merits than upon their probable influence on the next presidential election. And, in addition to this, it will probably be found, if their present institutions last, that they have subjected themselves to a series of much worse selections, and will have their Republic presided over by a less able and less creditable succession of men than if the Chief Magistrate had been chosen by the Legislature.

'It is but just to acknowledge that this very questionable provision was introduced in obedience to the important principle of preventing the Legislature from encroaching on the province of the Executive. The object was to make the President independent of the Legislature. It was feared that if he were appointed and could be turned out by them, he would be their mere clerk, would exercise no judgment and assume no responsibility of his own, but simply register the decrees of a body unfit to conduct the business of government in detail. There was, however, a means of avoiding this which would have been perfectly effectual. They might have given to the Chief of the Executive the power of dissolving the Legislature, and appealing afresh to the people. With this safeguard, they might have left to the Assembly the uncontrolled choice of the Head of the Executive, and the power, by a vote of dismissal, of reducing him to the alternative of either retiring or dissolving the Chamber. The check which, under this arrangement, the Legislature and the Executive would exercise reciprocally over one another, and the reluctance which each would feel to proceed to an extremity, which might end in their own downfall instead of their rival's, would in ordinary cases be sufficient to restrain each within the constitutional limits of its own authority. Instead of this, it is to be feared that by placing face to face an Assembly and a First Magistrate, each emanating directly from popular suffrage, and each elected for a term fixed, only capable of being abridged by death or resignation, the Assembly have organised a perpetual hostility between the two powers, replete with dangers to the stability of the Constitution. For if the President and the National Assembly should hereafter quarrel, there may for three whole years be no means by which either can relieve itself from the hostility of the other, except by a *coup d'état.* In addition to these considerations, an Executive chosen by a select body, and armed with the power of dissolving the Legislature, would probably be a more effectual check than any second Chamber upon the conduct of an Assembly engaged in a course of hasty or unjust legislation. An eminent politician, the leader of a great party, and surrounded by the *élite* of that party as his Ministers and advisers, would have more at stake in the good conduct of public affairs, would be more practised and skilful in judging of exigencies, would apply himself to his task with a much deeper sense of permanent responsibility, and, as a consequence of all this, would be likely to carry with him a greater weight of opinion, than an Assembly of two or three hundred persons, whether composed of English lords or of the elective representatives of French or American democracy.'

IV.

I had designed to add here some further discussion of the defect pointed out in the above extract from Mr. Mill—namely, the election of the President by the people. But my friend, Mr. Karl Blind, has called my attention to an article which appeared some years ago in a German Republican Magazine, which deals with this point so forcibly that I insert it, and the letter with which it is accompanied, in lieu of any remarks of my own:—

'We,' writes Karl Blind, 'who struggle for the People's cause in Europe, often turn our eyes towards the land of your birth, where the imprescriptible Rights of Man have first been proclaimed. Since the stain of slavery has been wiped from the American shield, and the States Rights' doctrine been made to yield before the Union, our sympathies for the great Republic have increased in depth and extent.

'The very warmth of the friendship we entertain towards America, makes us often ponder upon what we believe to be the flaws and faults of her Constitution. Ever since I have thought upon Republican questions, it has seemed to me that a head magistrate, elected outside of the legislative power, and invested with great privileges, is a danger to any free Commonwealth.

'To appoint, in the name of the sovereignty of the people, a Legislative Assembly, and then to appoint, once more in the name of the sovereignty of the people, a President of the Republic, both of whom may claim to be the expression of the popular will, is, in my opinion, illogical in theory and may turn out a snare to freedom. It is organising a constitutional conflict by constitutional machinery. It is setting up two rival powers which may clash at any moment. I believe this danger to exist, not only in old countries, with strong vestiges of monarchical tradition, which have recently adopted the Republican form, but also in new countries where a Conservative class is forming, which cares more for the enjoyment of rapidly gained wealth than for civic dignity, and the arduous political duties connected with it.

'A President who can boast of originating from a vote of the nation at large, is apt to think that he, in his single person, represents far more the nation than does an assembly composed of contending parties, each member of which is only chosen by a fraction of the people. If such a President has, in addition, large privileges in virtue of his office, he easily degenerates into what, among German Republicans, is called "*ein König im Frack*"—a King in a dress-coat.

'Hence, I hold that the true Republican way of appointing an Executive is, to select, out of the legislative power, a body of men chosen for a short time, invested with limited powers, the head man of whom is not re-eligible during a certain lapse of time, and who all are continually responsible to the representative assembly which is the source of their tenure of office.

'This is an opinion which, I think, I may safely say, is shared by the vast majority of German Republicans. It is an opinion which I have expressed so far back as the time of our Revolution, and repeated ever since in numerous writings. Of more recent utterances I will only add to this letter a few passages from a programme in the first number of the *Deutsche Eidgenoss* (" The German Republican ") of March 15, 1865—a programme to which many of the best and foremost men of our party have given their hearty assent':—

. . . 'The Constitution of the United States, however excellent in other respects, still bears, in some measure, the traces of the monarchical traditions of Europe. According to truly Republican principles, the executive power ought to originate from the legislative power, and continually remain responsible to it. But in America the President is appointed by an electoral act *outside* of the popular representation. He therefore stands on a level with the latter; maybe, in opposition to it; in a certain degree, even above it.

'Such a provision is only void of danger if the character of the man so appointed contains all guarantees of trustworthiness. It is difficult, however, to look into the human heart. The Constitution of a Republic should consequently be so framed, that it acts as a strong check and preventive against every despotic inclination.

'The disadvantages of the mode of election in the United States are only mitigated in so far as the appointment of a Chief of the Commonwealth is brought about by an election with two degrees. Even this feeble protection against certain surprises—such as have sometimes occurred in the history of Free States—a Republican party in America, which otherwise belongs to the most advanced, proposed to abolish! In the name of "Radicalism," the Cleveland Convention demanded that, in future, the election of a President should be accomplished by the direct vote of the masses. This desire is in direct contradiction to a wise Republican theory. We have seen the result of such a direct vote in France, in 1848. Through the conflict which broke out, in consequence of such a procedure, between the Legislative and the Executive, a Usurper made his way to arbitrary rule.

'In Switzerland, wiser counsels prevailed. According to Article 60 (of the Constitution of 1848), the supreme power is exercised by the national representation—the so-called *Bundes-Versammlung*. The character of the country being a federative one, this national representation is of a twofold nature : there is the *National-Rath* (House of Deputies of the People), elected by the population at large; and the *Stände-Rath* (Senate), appointed by the cantons, as such. Both parts of the national representation, in joint session, appoint the President of the Federal Council ; and he, strictly speaking, is nothing but a chairman *pro tem.* of an executive body which has been elected by the national representation, and is responsible to it.

' This is the true pyramidal form of a popular Commonwealth. . . . .

' The Federal Council (*Bundes-Rath*), i.e. the Executive of the Confederation (*Eidgenossenschaft*), is composed of seven members. The duration of its tenure of office is three years. Every Swiss who is eligible for the House of Deputies—that is, who has the suffrage and does not belong to the clerical order—is eligible for the Federal Council. Out of the seven members of that Executive— which is simply a parliamentary committee—the national representation appoints one member as a president and another as a vice-president. The president and vice-president are appointed for one year. After a year has elapsed, they are not reeligible to the same office for the following twelvemonth. If the House of Deputies is renovated by fresh elections, the Executive also must be elected afresh.

'These provisions are more radical than the corresponding ones of the American Constitution. Nevertheless, they are so framed that the passions of the whole mass of the people are not stirred up by the question of the headship of the Republic—that is, by a question of ambition. America has a Presidency for four years, and all the turmoil and unhealthy excitement connected therewith. Switzerland has simply a Chairmanship for one year in her Federal Council; but, owing to the truly Republican mode of election, the appointment is always made with the utmost quiet.'

The *Deutsche Eidgenoss* was edited by Karl Blind, with the co-operation of Dr. Louis Büchner, Georg Fein, Ludwig Feuerbach, Ferdinand Freiligrath, M. Gritzner, sen., General Ernst Haug, Friedrich Hecker, Theodor Mögling, K. Nauwerck, Theodor Olshausen, Dr. Gustav Rasch, Emil Rittershaus, General Franz Sigel, F. W. Schlöffel, Arnold Schlönbach, Gustav Struve, J. D. H. Temme, N. Titus, and others.

V.

It is most melancholy now to read the few notes preserved to us of the debates in the Convention which framed the American Constitution, relating to the formation of an Executive. It is plain that though the Colonies were fresh from a revolution which had been rendered necessary by the oppressive course of Great Britain, they still had a superstitious respect for the organic forms of that country. There were not wanting indeed some powerful voices which were raised in warning when it was proposed to raise to the Headship of the Republic an official who would necessarily be clothed with powers which the King of England would never dream of claiming, and struggled to entrust the administration of the laws to a responsible committee or cabinet of citizens; but they were not able to prevail against the superstition that since every nation must have a head, that head must consist of a single person. The monarchical germ was adopted into the Constitution by a majority of seven States against three, the great State of New York being in the minority, and consequently outweighed by four States which, taken together, were not its equal in population or importance; so that, if the Constitution of the American Republic had become organic law on Republican principles, the Executive would not now consist of an individual.

It was a mild-seeming ghost of a King, this Presidency, when it stood asking admission into the Constitution, and it was invested with the air of a progressive step; for there were other propositions which aimed to make the Executive the life-long office of one man, to render his negative absolute, and otherwise to make him a complete despot. But as the powers of the Executive were gradually arranged, the ghost put on flesh and blood and sinew. For it was evident that if the Executive were pledged to carry the laws into effect, he must have the appointment of his own agents, and entire control over them. They were the fingers of his hand. This implied the enormous power of patronage whose abuse has been the scandal of the American Government.

Every evil apprehended by those who hesitated to give any individual such enormous power has come to pass. Offices have been unnecessarily multiplied in order that Presidents might reward their friends, or gain support for the future, by filling such with influential persons. The President takes care, on entering office, to identify the interest of each village politician throughout the Union with the prolongation of his dynasty. It has become the settled rule of every President, upon his election, to remove nearly every official in the Government. Every post-office in America changes hands, every Ambassador and Consul is recalled; and, in order that the new President may reward those who have, and punish those who have not supported him, hardly a member of the American Civil Service—none in any important post—can ever remain longer than four years, or just long enough to have gained a proper knowledge of his office and duties. Setting aside the expensiveness of this presidential principle, that 'to the victors belong the spoils,' and apart even from the continual accession of crudity to replace experience implied in it, there is even a worse result in the temptation it offers every office-holder to devote his four years' tenure simply to money-making, in the face of a sure and speedy discharge. Why need he study his official duties thoroughly, who is to leave them so soon as he has mastered them ? And how can he be independent who holds his office under the vigilant eye of a master who can dismiss him in a moment ? Mr. Motley, the historian, holds a private conversation concerning the betrayal by President Johnson of the national confidence, and he is discharged from his post at Vienna by telegram.

How ludicrous that of all the hundred thousand officers in the Civil Service of free America there is not one who has opposed the re-election of Grant! While the unofficial public men of the country have been divided in a way quite unprecedented, and parties thrown into confusion, the holders of office, including the distinguished representatives of the United States in foreign capitals, present an absolutely unbroken phalanx for the power that feeds them!

No doubt a fair proportion of these would be for the re-election of the chief officeholder in any case; but that there would be a similar unanimity, had they all been private citizens, is inconceivable.

VI.

But besides the evils which many of the founders of the American Republic dreaded from the power lodged in one man, others equally serious have been developed in the process of time, of which the most far-seeing among them seems to have had no presentiment.

The first of these evils to be evolved was the degree to which a President, chosen for a certain term of office, can set aside the will of the country in spirit, without clearly violating it in the letter. It is doubtful whether the larger part of legislation may not lie in the spirit in which a law is carried out, rather than in the enactment itself. The ways in which an Executive may defeat the purpose of a law, while affecting to sustain it, are manifold—by delays, by appointing incompetent agents, or by entrusting the law to such as are hostile to it. A law may, in the majority of cases, as well not be passed at all as given over to be administered by its foes instead of its friends. Where a President clearly violates the law, or refuses to execute it, he is indeed liable to impeachment; but impeachment can take cognisance only of very gross derelictions, and the partisan Chief can generally take care to avoid committing technical offences in carrying out his will. The only possible surety that Executive Power shall administer the law in harmony with its spirit, and in accord with the country, is that it shall be responsible to the Legislature, and, while able to appeal to the suffrages of the people for support against any act, compelled to abdicate if the law be sustained. The strength of England lies in the fact that by its Constitution a change of policy involves a change of administrators. One of the most serious weaknesses of the American system is, that the Administrator is during his term practically irresponsible: he remains ruler for years, it may be, though the largest majority in both Houses of Congress may have condemned his policy.

To the late President Pierce Congress assigned the task of seeing that the inhabitants of the vast territory of Kanzas should at the polls adopt a Constitution in which the vexed question of the admission or non-admission of slavery therein should be finally determined by ballot. The emigrants who had settled Kanzas being by a large majority from the free States, it became clear that by even a proximately fair vote the free-State men would prevail. But President Pierce—a pro-Slavery partisan elected by pro-Slavery votes—actually encouraged civil war in Kanzas rather than have it organised on the basis of freedom. He protected Southern ruffians in armed attacks upon all who attempted to vote for freedom, and declined to interfere with the wholesale burning by them of the villages and homes of the Northern emigrants. The free-State men were compelled to accept the wager of battle, and their cause triumphed only at such terrible cost.

Under the administration of the late President Johnson, the virtual immunity of the Executive was completely proved. Johnson simply snapped his fingers in the face of Congress, as its laws fell one after another at his feet—dead letters. The power which looked upon him with loathing represented far more than two-thirds of the American people, and with all his resource of bribery he could not prevent each of his vetoes from being set aside by the requisite constitutional majority of two-thirds of both Houses of Congress. But the laws fell dead all the same. Congress impeached him, but it required two-thirds of the Senate for conviction; and when it became necessary to reduce the quarrel to legal forms, numberless loopholes presented themselves through which, with the assistance of administrative oil, enough of the very men who had been denouncing the President were induced to crawl away from the duty of dethroning him, thereby enabling this miserable man to remain at the head of the Government for the several remaining years of power which the unhappy death of Lincoln had thrown into his hands.

The vicious system of the Vice-Presidency unquestionably renders the American Republic especially liable to such evils as those just described. The Vice-Presidency is a comparatively idle office in itself. It is generally assigned by a party, in an honorary way, to some wing of it which has to be conciliated in order that its support of the Presidential candidate may be secured. Each Vice-President, consequently, is apt to represent some minority in the country which may nevertheless turn out to hold the balance of power in the election. The possibility that by the death of the President this man of the minority—generally a compromiser between antagonistic principles—may become the Chief Magistrate of the nation seems never to occur to any nominating convention, notwithstanding the terrible experiences which the United States has had from its accidental Presidents. Thrice within the current generation the American people have elected Presidents to carry out each a certain policy, and at their death have seen Vice-Presidents promoted to press the reverse policy in the most high-handed manner. The Mexican War, the execrable Fugitive Slave Law, and the villanies of Andrew Johnson's administration too numerous to be catalogued here, are our Vice-Presidential monuments.

Yet it is difficult to see how this bad system can be avoided if the Presidency be preserved, without increasing the temptations of defeated parties to assassinate the President-elect, or else, in case of his demise, throwing the country into the turmoil of another election.

VII.

Another very serious evil resulting from the One-Man Power in America—an evil undreamed of by the framers of the Constitution—is, that it has been the means of perpetuating in the Republic that fiction of rank—and snobbery, its natural concomitant—which is admittedly the evil shadow of even the mildest Monarchy.

Nothing is more essential to a Republic than that there shall be perfect equality between its citizens, so far as artificial distinctions are concerned. The very meaning of America in the political history of the world is the insufferable character of class privilege, distinctions founded upon birth or wealth or race, all distinctions which do not faithfully represent moral or intellectual superiority. Admitting that a President really represents a certain moral or intellectual eminence—he is more apt to represent in recent times only a more absolute servility to some party, or an unassailable obscurity—no one can contend that he has not, in every case, been surrounded by many equals in those respects, or that he has not, in the large majority of instances, had superiors in character or in genius. It has never happened in America that any President has been a genius or a great scholar, though that country has not been deficient in really great men. But throughout the world some of the lustre which is recognised on the brows of royal personages is accorded to the President and his family. While the son and daughter of President Grant were recently receiving distinguished attention at the hands of royal and official personages in Europe—while purple carpets have been spread before palace doors lest their feet should come in contact with the earth—there have been in this same continent the son and daughter of an American thinker of worldwide reputation—one believed by many to be the greatest philosopher living—but their presence was unheralded and unknown, save in literary circles. It is this false lustre—false because quite irrespective of real merit—which is reflected in the Presidency. It is this that makes that office an object of such keen and all-absorbing competition.

The rendering of homage to any man without reference to the services of that man is in a Republic a wretched anomaly. Did the American Executive consist of a Council or Cabinet, with a First Minister as their Chairman, it might be indeed that that First Minister might be invested with some of the glory of a highest position. We can only approximate the best. A First Minister of the people, sharing only with his Council the powers of patronage and control, could not be courted by self-interest, nor could he monopolise all the splendours of headship. The evil would at least be reduced to a minimum. No longer courted for his individual power, no longer flattered for his position whether he fill it well or not, he would have a stimulus to win eminence by deserving it. That kind of eminence is real, and that alone should be possible in a Republic.

VIII.

I ask those Republicans who follow the favourite method of the indolent, and ask not what is in a thing, but how does it work, to look back upon the Presidential struggle just terminated in America after having deeply humiliated the friends of that nation and of Republicanism. It will, for sad reasons, be fresh enough in recollection for some time to come to afford the only compensation for its disgracefulness, by exhibiting the true physiognomy of the One-Man Power, as transmitted from its crumbling throne in Europe to sit upon the healthy heart of America.

I read in the letter of an Englishman who sits at Washington and observes the struggle, a paragraph worthy of being pondered. 'We have here,' he says, 'persons who tell you that the Republican experiment, and the ballot especially, is a failure; that prejudice, ignorance, or fraud determine the result; and they are ready to give you reasons why the whole system should be discarded. But, even if they could by possibility prove all they allege, there is something too exciting and attractive in the choice of a President for the Americans ever to give up that great national sport. It is to them what the Derby is to you over the water—a great race, in which now one and now the other competitor seems to be ahead.'

That many of the politicians at Washington like this Presidential struggle, as a political Derby, for its excitements, is possible; but I would fain believe that the majority of the people are represented rather by those who can never behold it without misgivings as to the system itself, even though they are such as this correspondent of the *Daily Telegraph* (September 26) describes—unable to discriminate between the Republic and the parasite which has climbed over it.

The quadriennial struggle has always been the means of discovering to the shuddering world the two men who, in the estimate of half their countrymen, are the most unmitigated scoundrels in America. Some little time ago the religious Revivalists of the metropolis of that country were triumphant over the conversion of a certain keeper of a den of infamy who was distinguished as 'The Wickedest Man in New York.' This rascal enjoyed the distinction, his conversion made him a lion, and for a time he made it pay. After a time some new sensation drew away attention from him, and, falling from grace, he recovered his place as the Wickedest Man. But the Presidential canvass has revealed that this individual is a mere pretender. The Wickedest Man had all along been occupying the position of chief editor of the *New York Tribune*. While seeming for more than the quarter of a century to be devoting himself to schemes for the welfare of mankind, he has been deeply plotting against every interest of his country; whilst apparently during the same period resisting human bondage, even to the extent of suffering from the savage assault of a slaveholding Congressman, he has really been training himself for the task of re-enslaving the emancipated negroes; while his paper has been aiding to expose and crush the official swindlers called the New York Ring, he has secretly been conniving with its frauds; in short, according to the President of the United States and his supporters, all that is dark and diabolical in America has at last been traced to one figure-head, and that the head masked under the serene blonde face of Mr. Horace Greeley!

On the other hand, the votes cast against Grant in the recent election but very partially indicate the extent of the belief that he has shown himself a man more fit for the execration of his countrymen than for elevation above them. Millions make the minority which pronounce him a base self-seeker, an ignoramus, and a sot!

It is thus an incidental result of this, as of every Presidential election, that whoever be chosen passes to the supreme power branded by nearly half of those he is to govern as a man more fit for the common gaol than for the Executive Mansion. Nearly half the nation must, for four years, bow to the rule of a man they have declared unworthy to be received in decent society!

IX.

Such furious denunciations, such hurtling of vile accusations, such deep curses, as have attended the Presidential race-course, move me to declare, as a Republican, that I would gladly exchange the office thus recklessly sought for a nominal throne like that of England, whose occupant should consent to be a mere antiquarian symbol. The cost of the Queen may be onerous, but it may be paid in money—the Presidential election costs, not only the same money, but the good fame of thousands of eminent men. In the Grant-Greeley canvass, besides the charges against the principals already alluded to, the most prominent supporters of each have been equally subjected to accusations affecting their personal honour. A dozen eminent Senators, and as many Representatives, have been charged with having received bribes in specified instances. The Vice-President of the United States has been denounced as having sold his official influence to a railway corporation for money. The Speaker of the House of Representatives stands accused of the same offence; and hundreds of politicians have had scandals made up, or raked up, to be sources of bitterness and distress to themselves and their families for the rest of their lives. Political agents have gone through the country, as it were, with buckets of tar, and with commands to blacken the character of every antagonist. And to this must be added the demoralisation of the people by that wholesale bribery which rarely fails to make each Presidential election a monument of fraud.

All this indicates the unhealthiness of such a competition in a Republic. It revives the bitterness of the old wars of succession in Europe. It would be impossible if the prize were only the privilege of doing patriotic service to the country. It would disappear if each candidate were aspiring simply to some tenth part of the glory which crowns a President, and even that to be associated with a preponderant amount of toil and responsibility.

X.

The notion of the need, or theoretical propriety, of individual headship in a nation is a superstition; and it cannot be too speedily discarded by Republicans who are, essentially, political rationalists.

The progress of enlightened freedom has demonstrated that it requires many individual heads to make the head of a nation. In the ratio in which just and wise government is attained, the Monarch—if one has been inherited—must fade into an historical emblem, must remain, if at all, only as the device of a flag, while the real sovereign advances in the Cabinet. It is in this combination of special capacities related to every national interest that the Republic must find the various cerebral functions necessary to constitute the head of a people.

DELUSIVE DIPLOMACY.

I.

ABOUT fifteen years ago, the American people began to feel it a scandal that its representatives should be appearing at foreign Courts in costumes which had no sort of relation to the institutions of their country. What had a plain Republic to do with a dress denoting homage to the pomp and glitter of royalty? So the edict went forth that the foreign representatives of the United States should appear in palaces or elsewhere only in the dress of Republican citizens. Consternation among the functionaries in question was the result. Curious stories went back to America of how one Foreign Minister was mistaken for a servant, another refused admission to a royal drawing-room, and how one and all appeared in the mediæval masquerade as black notes of admiration amid pictorial sentences.

If decorated door-keepers perceived that the Republicans in evening dress were out of place amid the Court dresses, those representatives no less felt themselves out of place; and loud were the complaints returned to Washington, and the entreaties that the privilege of wearing the more imposing costume might be restored. But the complaints were heard with smiles, and with a certain satisfaction that some check seemed to have been given to the usual transformation of American Republicans into snobs.

But during all that discussion it seems to have occurred to but few that the wearing of Court-costumes by Republican Ambassadors was an anomaly because the Ambassador himself was an anomaly. The privilege of passing four years in a foreign capital, with a substantial salary and nothing to do, was too attractive for Ambassadors and Ministers to write home the confession that they were shams. So they have continued to write home ponderous letters about European politics, essays on foreign Governments, and the like, for the perusal and enjoyment of the public printers who issue the annual volume of 'Diplomatic Correspondence.'

The revelation that the American Minister abroad is a sham has had to come from the foreign countries themselves, and the most notable exposure has been frankly made by the English Chancellor of the Exchequer, in his speech at Glasgow, on September 26, 1872. Referring to the Arbitration at Geneva, Mr. Lowe said:

'There is one observation that was forced upon me in the case of these negotiations, and that is this: The fact that the Senate of the United States is the body which must ultimately ratify every treaty forms a difficulty in the way of negotiations of the most dangerous and perplexing nature, and one that will, one day or another, unless it is corrected, involve the United States in the greatest possible difficulty. The great men who framed the Constitution of America thought—very sensibly, as it appears on the first blush of things—that it was quite right so important a matter as a treaty should receive the confirmation of the representatives of the people; but they failed to see what I may call the reflex action which such a principle induces. It is this, that when you negotiate with the Government of America you are not negotiating with a plenipotentiary at all. The persons who speak on behalf of the Queen's Government can bind the Government to what they say; but the American Government cannot bind the people of America, because there is always the consent of the Senate to be obtained. The consequence is, that the Senate is consulted whenever any point is raised; but the Senate is not always in session; and when it is in session it is not, as a deliberating Assembly, bound by opinions given without it; and consequently one side is bound by what it proposes, while the other is at liberty to change it constantly. It really involves this, that in these matters the Senate should be consulted, and should give its opinion at every step, and that is the way we must account for the failure of the previous attempts at negotiation by Mr. Reverdy Johnson and Mr. Motley, because those were treaties negotiated by the Government, while the Senate had not given an opinion upon them, and had a right to repeal them. I mention this, not for the purpose of criticising the Government of America—which I know very well, from my own experience, is not very palatable to the Americans—but for our own guidance, because there are a great many gentlemen who think it would be a good plan that no treaty should be allowed to come into effect till it received the sanction of Parliament. No proposition can be more plausible, none more dangerous, because the effect would be that we should be obliged to obtain the sanction of Parliament before we negotiated, instead of after negotiating ; and anything like a public discussion, by a deliberative Assembly, of a treaty would be almost sure to be fatal to its conditions. I beg those who are naturally captivated by such a proposal to consider that when you say such an assent ought to be necessary, you cannot limit the functions of Parliament to that, but it involves the entanglement of Parliament as a party in the negotiations, and as a party to every step, which, in the case of a large deliberating body, is absolutely impossible.'

No doubt this criticism will be met in America with some star-spangled resentment, and some indignant screams from the national eagle; but any momentary humiliation that a thoughtful and honest Republican of the United States may feel that it should be left to a foreign statesman to call the attention of the world to so obvious a truth must be speedily lost in the sense of gratitude to the brave man who has had the courage and candour to do so with plainness and force.

II.

I will not pause here to consider whether it be true, as Mr. Lowe maintains, that satisfactory negotiations for treaties with foreign powers are incompatible with the anterior discussion of their conditions by a deliberative Assembly. It seems to me plain that in a rightly constituted Government a Council of Ministers, chosen by the Legislature and responsible to it, would be able to combine the advantages of representative deliberation with those of executive competency. Such a Council would be a Parliament in little, and would be a safe Commission to which some degree of legislative authority might be entrusted for exceptional purposes. It is a main advantage of the English Constitution that the Parliament may ratify a treaty and on the same day turn out the Ministry that made it. No Government will be likely under such circumstances to act in violation of the right or honour of the nation which it can only command by obedience.

Mr. Lowe has wisely refrained from pointing America to the method of England as the means of avoiding the dangers he foresees for her style of diplomacy. The adoption of such a method would imply a fundamental modification of the American Constitution. No man in the United States would consent to have himself bound by the action of any agent sent abroad by the President and responsible only to that most irresponsible of all officials. The President may appoint an Ambassador without even consulting those private clerks who are euphemistically called his Cabinet. His appointee will be invariably confirmed by the Senate, because otherwise the opposition would be subjected to retaliation when its own President should be elected and its own adherents be asking for senatorial confirmation to high offices. An appointment by the President must be an outrageously corrupt one for the Senate to refuse its consent to it. The Ambassador once appointed shares the irresponsibility of the Executive. And with a record of Presidents who have made Mexican Wars, Kanzas Wars, Slavehunting Bills, Filibustering Raids, and the like, it would be simple madness in the American people to consent that their policy toward other nations should be controlled by the word of an individual at Washington or his agent in foreign lands.

So long as the appointing power of the President remains without substantial check, the question in America will rather be how to extend to the representatives of the people a share in the treaty-making power now monopolised by the Senate, whose servility to the Executive in such matters has become almost normal.

A Republic can be able to deal freely and finally with other Governments when its Administration represents the Congress itself, in smaller dimension, and in perpetual session. The immediate responsibility of every functionary is its only security.

But beyond this there is a question of hardly inferior importance relating to the necessary attitude of a Republic towards the diplomatic method of monarchical countries. In its international affairs the question of form is of the utmost importance. America has decided that her foreign representatives shall not masquerade in costumes taken from the wardrobe of privileged classes. But these costumes are only symbols. Is it not even more inconsistent that a Republic shall join in the circle of diplomacy arranged by monarchs claiming the right to carry on bargains affecting the interests of their subjects without consultation with those subjects? The Republican diplomatist is necessarily a counterfeit of the real diplomatist. He is under false colours. But make him a reality —make him the extended hand of the Republic— and he is all the more out of place in the bazaar where the rights of peoples are bought and sold by crowned heads. It is difficult for the Republican to reside among such without catching some of their habits. The superstition which preserves diplomacy may very easily slide into the practice of duplicity which has been its historical physiognomy.

It is a central law of the Republic that it can have no 'Reasons of State.'

There may, indeed, arise cases where a Republic must have dealings with foreign countries. Avoiding all such negotiations with autocratic Powers as are inconsistent with the duty each Republic owes to humanity, refusing absolutely to become an ally of any oppressor against the denied rights of a people, there are, nevertheless, cases in which it may be necessary for the welfare of mankind that even autocratic Governments shall be recognised and dealt with. *Summum jus summa injuria.* But that such negotiations shall be as clean and just as possible, let the Republican Ambassador reside at home. If the Republic has anything to transact with a foreign nation, let its Messenger start with the spirit of his country still fresh upon him. Let him not be trained to smoothness of tongue and ingenuity in indirection in the atmosphere of aristocracies. Let the Republic select its wise and sufficient man for each such task as it may arise; let him go to the foreign capital as the voice and seal of his country; let him drive to the door of Cabinet or palace in his cab, transact his affair, and then return home.

CONCLUSION.

One of the ablest of the founders of the American Republic has left it on record that a considerable part of the Constitution of that country was passed by the Convention with undue haste, owing to an apparently trivial circumstance. The Convention was sitting in a crowded room, in a dusty city, and under the heat of midsummer. These disagreeable circumstances were rendered almost intolerable by the infliction of a plague of gnats, which so stung the distinguished gentlemen through the thin stockings in which their legs were encased in those days, that their attention could hardly be given to the weighty matters before them, and they were only too eager to compromise their differences, and hasten to their respective homes.

This little army of gnats, it is to be feared, was a formidable reinforcement to the reactionists of the Convention, and their stings have been felt throughout American history.

When America shall have swept away the old State limits, and divided her territory into equal electoral districts; when she shall have empowered every such district to govern itself in its local interests, and to obtain a share in guiding the nation at large; when every respectable minority shall have an influence in the Legislature proportionate to its numbers and ability; when every representative of the nation meets every other face to face in debate, in one Chamber and on equal terms; when there shall be no artificially eminent office or rank; when there shall be no imitation of alien systems at home or abroad—then will America be what it has never yet been, a Republic, and Republicanism throughout the world may then fearlessly consent to be judged by the character and working of Transatlantic institutions.